This Little Light Of Mine

Delores Finger Yarbough

iUniverse, Inc.
New York   Bloomington

This Little Light Of Mine

Copyright © 2010 Delores Finger Yarbough

All rights reserved. No part of this book may be used or reproduced by any means, graphic, electronic, or mechanical, including photocopying, recording, taping or by any information storage retrieval system without the written permission of the publisher except in the case of brief quotations embodied in critical articles and reviews.

iUniverse books may be ordered through booksellers or by contacting:

iUniverse
1663 Liberty Drive
Bloomington, IN 47403
www.iuniverse.com
1-800-Authors (1-800-288-4677)

Because of the dynamic nature of the Internet, any Web addresses or links contained in this book may have changed since publication and may no longer be valid. The views expressed in this work are solely those of the author and do not necessarily reflect the views of the publisher, and the publisher hereby disclaims any responsibility for them.

ISBN: 978-1-4502-0832-1 (pbk)
ISBN: 978-1-4502-0833-8 (cloth)
ISBN: 978-1-4502-0834-5 (ebk)

Printed in the United States of America

iUniverse rev. date: 3/1/2010

Contents

Foreword vii

Introduction ix

Chapter 1.   Jesus 1

Chapter 2.   A Positive Mission 8

Chapter 3.   He Resurrected Me 12

Chapter 4.   Beware Of Who Angels Are 19

Chapter 5.   Nothing But The Grace Of God 23

Chapter 6.   God Can Do Any Thing 28

Chapter 7.   Is The Beauty Within Or Without? 32

Chapter 8.   When He Opens The Door 36

Chapter 9.   Promises, Promises, Promises 39

Chapter 10.   Sin and Bear Its Results 43

Chapter 11.   God's Grace In Action 48

Chapter 12.   God Has The Last Word 52

Chapter 13.   You Can Live Without a Man 56

Chapter 14.   Why Don't You Go to Church? 65

Chapter 15.   How do You Feel About Tithing? 69

Chapter 16.   God is not through with me Yet 72

Chapter 17.   The Cross Makes the Difference 75

Chapter 18.   Thy Word is Everlasting 79

Chapter 19.   Know The Truth 80

Chapter 20.   Get Ready, Get Ready, Get Ready 85

Chapter 21.   A Silhouette of a Angel 87

Chapter 22.   Blessed Assurance 92

Chapter 23.   To Obey Is To Win 95

About the Author: 99

Foreword

Let your light so shine before men, that they may see your good works, and glorify your Father which is in heaven. Matthew 5: 16

THIS LITTLE LIGHT OF MINE

This book is a small way the Lord has anointed me to write to reach those who will not pick up a Bible, but will read another book. In a simple way to reach others with the Good News. In this book you will find the truth written in simple language that can be easily understood. This book has been written for your understanding with out having a Theological approach to the word of God. It is written for plain, simple, basic truths explaining the most important facts. The way to repent, turn from sin, receive Salvation and follow Christ. In addition it should encourage you to study the word of God further. *2 Timothy 2: 15 Study to shew thyself approved unto God, a workman that needeth not be ashamed, rightly dividing the word of truth.*

My prayer is the Lord Jesus Christ Bless this book to be a blessing to all that read it and harden not their hearts, but except the word that leads to a life productive in Christ. In this book I have given you Holy Scriptures that will lead you to Christ that you might be saved. Scriptures that will able you to see the light, and grow in the Lord. It is my prayer also that in reading this book you can say it has given you light, peace, joy, and a priceless walk in love with the Lord.

Introduction

It is so wonderful to be a child of God. I want to tell the best thing that has happened to me in my life is when I saw the light, and asked the Lord to save my soul. ***Luke 14: 23 And the Lord said unto the servant, Go out into the highway's and hedges, and compel them to come in, that my house may be filled.*** This is my desire for all that read this book to be able to say this while in the land of the living. It is your decision to make your choice here and now while you are alive as some people say and kicking. The world is in critical condition and we know not weather we will live to send our grandchildren to Collage or wake up in the morning to go to work. If you want to face reality do you see any difference in today's world, and the world in the Bible days of Sodom and Gomorrah. Sin is prevalent, sex is glorified not God. Wars and rumors of war is today's headlines. There is little trust in people in high places, they have sold us down the drain for the power of money. Where is our mothers love, the only thing we could depend on; now it has turned around mothers are killing their own children. Our only true love is God's love.

This book is written to let you know there is a way out. Jesus is the way the truth and the light. He is the only way. Did you know every eye shall see Jesus? He judges you at the time of your death. He knows if you are one of his and you will live with him Eternally. If you have not repented of your sins you do not belong to Him, You will hear Him say depart ye worker of iniquity, and you will be sent down to Hell. All people will see Jesus, but none but the pure in heart shall see God. This book is to help you find the way, and let you see the light as He is the Light.

1 John 4: 15 Whosoever shall confess that Jesus is the Son of God, God dwelleth in him and he in God.

Chapter 1

JESUS

Now I would not advise you to close this book because you have opened to the first page to discover Chapter 1 is entitled Jesus. The name is emphasized in large print. There is a reason for this, that reason is because of who He is. His name is above all other name: ***Acts 4: 12 Neither is there Salvation in any other: for there is none other name under heaven given among men, whereby we must be saved.*** This should be enough for you too never allow any one, anything, any devil, *make you think Jesus does not exist and is not important.* ***Matthew 1: 21 And she shall bring forth a son and thou shalt call his name Jesus for he shall save his people from their sins.*** I would not have you to think there is no value in the name of Jesus or that He has no particular meaning in your life or to you. I want to let you know in this Chapter 1 how important Jesus is in your life and mine.

In this Chapter I, hopefully you will receive an insight of just who Jesus is and in the process proof by the word of God. Jesus is able to do in your life and what he has done for me in my life. You have no life if you don't have Jesus, For he has given you life on earth and he has given you life in heaven. For if it were not for Jesus you would not be able to have life in heaven. He died for you to have that life for He died on Calvary for your sins to give you Eternal life. Do you know any one that would do anything for you with out you giving him something? He died for you it didn't cost you anything, he died so that you can live after you die, in Eternity with Him, and be free of all suffering of this world.

John 1: 1- 5 In the beginning was the Word an the Word was with God, and the Word was God The Word was in the beginning with God. All

things were made by him: and without him was anything made that was made.

Jesus is the Word, Jesus was with God from the beginning. Jesus is the way, the truth and the light you are going to be glad when you find out more about Jesus, you will love Him and want to hear more about Him. He will be your all and all the more you know of him, the more you will let him mean to you. He is everything to you and to all people.
Hallelujah!! aren't we on the road to filling the joy in praising him. Knowing this is something we all can shout about, but let's go on, he gets better the more we discover about Him and what He has done for you and I.

In this day and time of cultural civilization, people are leaving the real meaning of the Christmas Holiday and Christmas Season out. I feel the urge to warn you not to let the devil nor anyone else who tries to persuade you not to respect our Christmas Holiday that is all about HESUS and not toys.
Christmas : for this is the time of the Birth of Jesus, God in Human flesh.
John 1: 12-13 But as many as received him, to them gave he power to become the son's of God, even to them that believe on his name. Which were born not of blood, nor of the will of the flesh, nor of the will of man, but of God. Can you imagine a virgin having a baby before you have known a man. God did it. Oh how great thou art.
Christmas is our highest Holy time in our Christian experience the time of our Lord Jesus Christ Virgin birth. There are early records to prove this event. It might not be about that exact date, the time of the year according to godly men who give us the date December 25th. Its more important for you to know that God designed this time for Jesus to be born. Every thing is set up according to God's timing. The Birth of Jesus was after everything was completed on this earth and the time was right for His birth. The same is your birth, your life, your coming to Christ, and your death. The important thing is it is Christ Birthday, a day our Jesus was born according to the scripture.
Luke 2: 7, 11, And she bought forth her first born son, wrapped him in swaddling clothes; and laid him in a manger; because there was no room for them in the inn. For unto you is born this day in the city of David a Saviour, which is Christ the Lord.

Luke 2:21 And when the eight days were accomplished for the circumcising of the child, his name was called Jesus, which was so named of the angels before he was conceive in the womb. The Shepherds that were given the news that night celebrated his birth by praising God and saying Glory to God in the highest, and on earth peace, good will toward men. They went to where he was and praised him, and eight days later he was circumcised His name JESUS was given before birth. Christmas has the word Christ in it. Christmas is all about Jesus. He was God born in human flesh who experienced all our human emotions in all of life's aspects. Jesus Christ (the anointed one)

Do not let anyone take the meaning of this high holy time of Jesus birth. Followed by His holy life, His record of Miracles, of Healing, and of His sacrificial death for our sins. It is becoming more common to hear politicians and people in high places say we should not include the name of Jesus in prayer in our schools, public speaking places, praying, or teaching. The cross of Jesus our symbol and the Bible is also being rejected as he said Everything shall pass away but the word of God.

Philippines 2: 9 –11 Wherefore God also hath exalted him, and given him a name which is above every name: That at the name of Jesus every knee should bow, of things in heaven, and things in earth, and things under the earth. And every tongue should confess that Jesus Christ is Lord, to the glory of God the Father

Some have the audacity to boast they will run their position of the country on the Law of man an not on the Bible. Before these big politicians talk about what they won't do. I think they should think it was on the word of the Bible that sat up the Law of the people of this America. This concerns me what is the hope of the stability of our nation if we will put law over God our creator and lawmaker. Should we forget this county was founded on the word of God? Our forefathers acknowledge the position God should have in our world and country as above all Humanity in so much that they put this recognition on our legal tender, (in God we trust). It frightens me to hear of this happening for I realize these and many other frightening things are about to come upon us who believe they have power over all. Jesus Christ is soon to come back. HE is coming as King of Kings and Lord of Lords it is written that HE is the power of the world. Tribulation will come upon us before then. It is written in the bible for all to read.

In one of my other Chapters I describe how I was so sick I thought I was going to die. I can truthfully tell you how glad I am that I knew Jesus as Savior and my Lord. I called upon the name of Jesus and he raised me up from the deathbed. I will praise him not only on Christmas but everyday he allows me to arise in the morning with breath in my body. I will worship adore and praise his holy name. No one will convince me to refrain from speaking or proclaiming the name of JESUS for no other name has done and will do what

Jesus has done for me and is still doing. No other name I know. I want the name of Jesus to be in my mouth when I take my last breath.

I endeavor to bring a few more points to expound the name of JESUS further, Could I ask you a personal question? Do you know of any one who would give his life for you to be able to live forever? Would your mother who loves you probably more than anyone you know of maybe? father, brother, son, or friend? No not one. It is likely for you will find any one to give his or her life for you, regardless to the situation. I am trying to give you a few points to prove your need to be a true believer in Jesus Christ him and his word. I want you to think of his powerful life while he lived on earth. How he performed miracles, healed the sick, returned site to the blind, walked on water, preached the word, lived a perfect life. I like it when he said he was about his fathers' business. I like it after his birth, he had a few years to do the work of his father. He was baptized of John and began his ministry. He was kicked out of the synagogue while preaching the word of God. Sound like today don't you think?. the Pharisees did not want him to preach about JESUS, and about a believer in the word of God who was not a JEW he was kicked out of church. The same devil who hates the name of JESUS and who has not love of God did not want the name of JESUS mentioned in the schools. He was kicked out of schools, He was kicked out the home. In all JESUS has made the difference in each one of the important impact of each one of these important places. One day he will meet JESUS face to face and will be sent to HELL forever.

His first miracles including changing water into wine to raising Lazarus from the dead, healing the sick and afflicted. Walked on water, Calmed the sea, opened the blinded eyes, cast out demons, fed the multitude, died on Calvary for our sins, rosed from the dead on the third day, Ascended into heaven, seated on the right hand of his Father making intercession for us. During this period of time in his life it was such an important time to us. The same miracles he performed then he is still performing them now. At this time it is important to have the faith to believe without it you will miss the miracle the Lord has for you and you want to blame the Lord for not performing a miracle for you. This is the plan for Satan to use to deceive you further in other things.

Is there any one in the history of our world that ever worked Miracles like Jesus worked? No, we have people that worship Buddha, Mohammed, and many other religious leaders who in history have not accomplished working miracles why because they were not of the deity of Jesus and have not the power of God. I am glad they can't work miracles because if they could they would be against working one for me. Would any one of them die for you or me and for your sins that we might have life everlasting? In today's world you have people who hate the Christians and are killing them for their belief.in JESUS. This same as been done down through the centuries before for the cause of JESUS CHRIST.

Of all the reasons we should love Jesus our first and foremost reason should be that he gave His life for us that we might have Everlasting Life. *1 John 4: 2 Hereby know ye the Spirit of God, Every spirit that confessing JESUS CHRIST is come in the flesh is of Cod.*

John 6: 40 And this is the will of him that sent me, that every one which seeth the Son, and believth on him, may have everlasting life: and I will raise him up at the last day. I am so glad I have that hope within my soul. Jesus is the only one who went to that cruel death on Calvary for all of our sins, healing and everything we need to live holy before God. He went to the cross in obedience to his father that I we might have eternal life. *Luke 23: 33 And when they were come to the place, which is called Calvary, there they crucified him, And the malfactors, one on the right hand and the other on the left.*

We have touched upon the birth and death of Jesus now if Jesus did not arise from the grave on the third day we would not have the promise of Eternal Life. He arose from the dead with power. *Luke 24:6-7 46 He is not here, but is risen: remember how he spoke unto you when he was yet in Galilee, Saying the Son of man must be delivered into the hands of sinful men, and be crucified, and the third day rise again. And said unto them, Thus it is written, and thus it behoved Christ to suffer, and to rise from the dead the third day. And that repentance and remission of sins should be preached in his name among all nations; beginning in Jerusalem. And ye are witness of these things.*

Recently in the news there has been reported a man who is an Archeologist looking for notoriety and fame states he has discovered the tomb of Jesus, his wife, and his two children. He could have found a tomb with Jesus name on it but it is not our Jesus Christ. Our Bible does not give us information that our Jesus was ever married or had any children. In that day and time many people named their children and men were named Jesus. Expect things like this coming to the surface at this time when the Lord is soon to come. Men are trying to disprove the word of God and disprove the Christian belief in

Jesus Christ and his Diety. The word of God tells us the world and all therein shall pass away but the word of God will last forever.

What a debt he paid for all of us. Jesus paid it all, all to Him I owe, sin has left a crimson stain, but He washed it white as snow. I cannot end this Chapter 1 without what I conclude to be a happy ending for all of us. He is still doing something for us, He is leading those who live for Him, by his Holy Spirit. He is seated on the right hand side of God the father making intercession for all of us. *John 2: 1-2 My little children these things write I unto you, that ye sin not and if any man sin, we have an advocate with the Father, Jesus Christ the righteous: And he is the propitiation for our sins: and not for ours only but also for the sins of the whole world.*

I will elevate the name of JESUS. He loved me so much that when I was going astray, he opened my eyes to let me see Him. He paid the supreme sacrifice on Calvary he died for all my sins. On the third day He arose again, with the power over death, the grave and hell. Jesus paid it all to him I owe, Sin had left a crimson stain, but He washed me white as snow. You have heard the simple points about Jesus but you will never know all about Jesus until you know Him for your self in the pardon of your sins. Right now is the time to start to know Him. Repeat these words right now and mean them from your heart Lord forgive me from all my sins.

Say these words; Jesus I am a sinner I believe you will save me from my sins I sincerely ask you. I am asking you to come into my heart and save me. I need to be saved. I want to turn away from my sins, but I need you. Forgive me of all my sins. Now that you have asked Jesus to save you believe that you are saved. You will not have the desire to do the sinful things you use to do. Turn away from your sinful habits. Put that woman (man) you are not married to out of your life, empty your bar and make it into a library, you can do all things through Christ that strengthen you He will help you. If your heart is sincere JESUS will change your mind so that you will no longer have the desire to do what you use to do. He will take all the other desires away from and you find you can no longer have the desire to do then.

You must get unto a Gospel preaching church where you can learn the Bible and more of Jesus so you can live a life that is pleasing to the Lord Jesus. Commit your life over to Jesus and let him make of you what he will.

[Song]
He's real, real, he's so real to me
He's real, real, he's so real to me
you can't make me doubt him
I know too much about Him
that is why I love him so, he's so real to me.

He's the Lilly of the Valley
He's my Bright and Morning Star
He' the Light of the World
He's the Rose of Sharon,
He's my Jehovah Rapha The Lord that Healeth
He's my Jehovah Raah he Lord My Shepherd
He's my Jehovah Jireh The Lord will Provide
He's my Jehovah Nisi The Lord Our Banner
He's my Jehovah Sholom The Lord Our Peace
He's my Jehovah Shammah The Lord is Present
My All and All

Matthew 19: 26 But Jesus beheld them, and said unto them, With men this is impossible; but with God all things are possible.

Chapter 2

A POSITIVE MISSION

The December cold weather was mixed with rain and snow this is the kind of weather old folks would say people should stay out of. This weather is no good for you no matter if you are young or old. This weather will chill you through and through after the chill then a temperature soon your nose will start running. You will become congested and you might have an Asthmatic attack now you have trouble on your hands.

It does not stop there it can trigger your heart to start beating irregular from a build up of fluid around it. Now you begin a game call blood pressure climbing up higher. You know you have to get up and go to a minimum wage job to keep your car in gas, get your hair done don't forger your nails and bottled water. You get to stand in on spot from five to eleven with cold air blowing down from a ventilator. You learn to take abuse from ungodly, evil, angry, frustrated liars used by Satan to destroy your joy. You don't like going to work but you need the money. The cold you have has taken control of your head, ears, nose, and chest and is winning because you can't sleep. So get up and get go knowing if it was not for the Lord giving me the strength I could not make it.

I always enjoy the New Years watch service at my church maybe I should have stayed at home but I remember I use to go out to parties to celebrate. but Christ has made a change in my life, and now I go to church because I love to praise the Lord who is the lover of my soul. While enjoying the service I had a bad coughing spell and could not stop. People were so kind to bring me water, cough drops, but nothing seemed to help I was so sorry to disturb the service. While I was coughing I notice I was having a Asthma attack. I had not had a Asthma attack for over a year. I could not pinpoint the reason for the attack, but with prayer I stopped coughing and was able to enjoy the rest of the service.

The next day I found myself coughing more and more I went to a clinic for medication but was told there was no one there to give me medication. I called the Hospital and they told me to come to the Emergency. I did not like going to the Emergency because I knew I would have a long wait. To my surprise I was taken right in. I was coughing and having an Asthma attack. The large room and beds were full of sick people. They sat me in a chair in a little alcove and began giving me the inhaling treatment for Asthma. The coughing continued after the first treatment so they gave me the second treatment. After the third treatment I had a reaction which cause me to shake all over I didn't know what was going on I was shaking so hard I couldn't talk for shaking.

The nervous convulsing like shaking continued for hours I asked the Doctor what happened to me that cause me to shake like that he told me the treatments were to close together and the medication was to strong that's what caused the uncontrollable shaking. After hours passed the shaking subsided and I began to feel better. A nurse came to me and saw I was improved from the reaction and told me she was going to move me into a bed, I told her I was feeling so much better and I would be going home soon, for you have people that could use the bed. She told me Oh no we will find a bed for you soon. The headache and coughing continued. I prayed and told the Lord I am not as sick as some of these people are let me go home so someone can have my bed.

It didn't take long before the nurse came and led me to a bed, I would have missed it because it was in a smaller space than the alcove. I climbed up onto the bed with one leg and foot hanging out of the bed with both shoes on. It seems to me as soon as I hit that bed nurses, doctors and lab people pounced on me for this test and that test blood was taken out of both arms at the same time. I was given a x-ray of the chest, and abdomen. I guess you would say I got the attention I needed. I had a great urgency to pray for all the people I saw in the emergency area.

I was so tired I went to lie down when I heard someone speak to me in a feeble tone of voice saying you must have Asthma like me, I replied yes I am having an Asthma problem but I am going home very soon I will be fine. I had not looked to see who spoke to me, but thought I would take a look. The lady kept talking it was hard to make out what she was saying. I looked into the next bed and saw a lady who looked to be in grave condition. Her color was gray and her breathing was labored. I had no doubt in my mind she was put there to die. She said to me I am so glad you are here I don't want to be by myself. I didn't quite know how to take her conversation there seemed to be an urgency in her voice. I must talk to you she continued I didn't know what she was going to talk about, but I knew what I was going to talk about. I would talk about the one I knew could help her for he is the one I loved and his name is Jesus.

I told her I would pray for her but every time I started to go to her someone would come and do something to me, or they would do something to her. After a short let up I tried to rest, I closed my eyes but it hit me you have not prayed for her yet. I asked the Lord to forgive me for being slow about praying for her. I got out of the bed and took a step to her bed I ask her if she believed in the Lord Jesus Christ, that he was born of a virgin, that he died on the cross for our sins, was buried and arose the third day., that he is seated on the right hand of his father. She told me that she believed and that she was a member of a Missionary Baptist Church. I did not know the church she mentioned for I was not acquainted with the churches in the city I wondered why she had no one there with her as sick as she was some one should have been there.

I began to pray for and the power of the Holy Ghost fell upon me and I stopped dead still, and the Lord spoke to me and said You are here at this place at this time to minister to this women, with my mouth opened I was like Oh my God I had never had this happened to me before. I wondered if I had said what the Lord had wanted me to say. A nurse was standing at the curtain waiting for me to finish praying for her then she entered and began to care for the women. ***Hebrew 13: 3 Let your conversation be with out covetousness and be content with such things as ye have: for he hath said, I will never leave thee, nor forsake thee.***

When the nurse left, the woman called me back to her side I could not make out what she was saying so I bent down to better hear what she was saying, she had oxygen going in her nose IV's running in her arm that's when she told me she had full blown AIDS and that her liver and pancreas was affected by it. She told me she knew the Lord had sent me to minister to her and pray for her healing. She also told me she was saved and believed in the healing power of the Lord. She also told me her name, but I didn't remember it, then she told me the name of her church a Missionary Baptist Church here in the city I did not recognize the name of the church. She pleaded with me not to leave her, I told her I would be there with you if I can, and that the Lord will never leave her. She told me I looked like an angel. Do you want to know something that was a humbling moment to me that the Lord would used me for this mission to this special person of his, at this particular time.

After a while she was moved, as they were moving her she asked the nurse if

I could go with her the nurse told her "no you are going to one place she will be going to another place". I was so glad to have prayed with her before she was moved because I would never see her again or know what happened to her. They were moving every one from the Emergency area to rooms in the Hospital. I thought they would send me home I figured it was finished what the Lord had for me to do, but the nurse told me my doctor wanted me to stay a few days and that I was going to a room with a bed. Well I was so glad I said at least I can put both feet and my whole body in the bed and sleep. The nurse told me my doctor wants to monitor my heart longer on a heart monitor and the room I am going to is the only one left with a heart monitor in it.

As they pushed my bed with me in it into the room I said Oh no another small close space. They hooked me up to a monitor, I felt so tired I said to myself I am going to try to get some sleep now. Just as I turned to put my head down on my pillow I saw the curtain that divided the patient in the bed next to mine sliding back so the person could see whom they just bought in. I looked over to see who was sliding the curtain open and to my surprise was the women I prayed for. She smiled at me and said I am so glad you are there. I prayed and ask the Lord to heal her I did not know what else to do. I cannot do anything for her because I was hooked up to the monitor and can't get up, I knew my job was not over yet with the lady.

I looked at her and her color had not changed she was still gray, but she seemed to be stronger. I wanted to be sure I didn't neglect giving her the word of God and making sure she had given her life over to the Lord. Too make sure I asked her again to repeat the sinners pray and asked her if it was well with her soul whenever the Lord would come for her she said it was. I told her now was the time to make her calling and election sure. *2 Peter 1:10*
Wherefore the rather, brethren, give diligence to make your calling and erection sure; for if ye do these things, ye shall never fall

After about six doctors and all the procedures they could put me through, I guess they felt it was time for them to release me and they sent me home, I was ready to go, but more important it was Gods' timing. As I was leaving I went over to say good by to the lady but was unable to get to her. There were doctors and nurses around her trying to get her to breath, I left the room thanking God for who he is, his goodness, his mercy, for the lady he had me to give his word too. I prayed for all the doctors and nurses that gave me care and were nice to me. Mainly I thanked Him for fulfilling the Possible Mission he put me on. *Jude 1:21- 22 Keep yourself in the love of God, looking for the mercy of our Lord Jesus Christ unto eternal life. and of some have compassion, making a difference.*

1 Peter 5:10 After that ye have suffered a while, make you perfect, establish, strengthen, settle you.

Chapter 3

HE RESURRECTED ME

At the time I am writing this in December 2004 I am not out of the woods yet, but my Faith has just gone into overdrive again. I see a little more light, I do not know what the title of this miracle testimony will be, but the Lord has not finished with me yet. I know when he gave me the title of this testimony it will exceed any awesome experiences I have experienced yet or could have conceived in my finite mind. He has not bought me out completely yet, but He is not letting me fall, I am still holding on to his unchanging hand and praying for strength only he can give me. I want to walk again I do not want to rely upon a cane or a wheelchair to be ambulatory.. I have had back injuries before times in my profession as a nurse I have had several back injuries, they would heal after a while with medication, but this injury from this truck running into me and at my age has done more damage then all the previous back injuries I have had to happen in my entire life. I have experienced this last time the pain in my back does not allow me to put any weight on my feet to take two or three steps at a time. I am waiting for the Lord to overpower me with his spirit enabling me to better realize or comprehend just what has happened to me during this invasion on my healthy state of body and mind.

I am willing to testify to what the Lord is bringing me through. I can say I would not want any one to go through these experiences of being ill to death. I can't wait to give these experiences of what I have come through with the help of the Lord. I feel as if I was not me going through this but some one else was in my body.

The only realization of all that is happening to me is that I know in whom I believed. I knew he is more than able to bring me through. *Jude 1: 24-2 Now unto him that is able to keep you from falling and present you faultless before the presence of his glory with exceeding joy, to the only wise God our Saviour, be glory and majesty, dominion and power, both now and ever. Amen* It is good to know the scriptures in times like these when you really need the word to bring you through.

Along with sever pain, my Diabetes was going haywire, eyesight failing, appetite was gone, I was just waiting to die. I recall weeks of insomnia night after night, being afraid to move because of the pain. I was going to die, things I could not shake off, thoughts that were so strange to me. At times I had dreams of things happening to me that were disturbing and unbelievable. I would wake up and sit straight up in my bed frightened and in a cold sweat. I never had anything like this to happen to me before in all my life. It seemed to me as if I was in half of my body I didn't know what to think about these strange situations that kept me in this state of horrified captivity, but I called on the name of Jesus all day and night, for weeks. *Psalms 119: 55.* **I have remembered** *thy name, O Lord,* **in the night, and have kept thy law.** I said I will hold on to the Lord who was the Author and Finisher of my Faith. Jesus spoke to me and said it is my Grace and Mercy that will bring you out of this illness.

This illness cause me to experience overwhelming anxious times which was totally new and different than my normal calm state of mine. I found it hard to hold on to my thoughts, precepts, belief, and faith in my God. I had to totally trust the Lord to lead and guide me through this time until he delivered me out. He knew my heart and because of His love for me God KEPT ME GOD KEPT ME. I felt like I was on the ropes and if I let go I would fall in a deep hole. I thought the Lord was going to let Satan have me when I let go, but the Lord held me up he kept me from falling He did not let me go. Glory Halleluiah. *Psalms 118: 9 -18.* I repeated these words the Lord gave me all night every night. *I shall not die, but live, and declare the works of the Lord. The Lord has chastened me sore: but hath not given me over unto death.* I found this scripture was my road map out of this. I kept repeating His word, promise, and His name Jesus. I held on them for dear life.

It seemed I was suspended in mid air. I thought Angels were on both side holding me up, I do believe it was the angels of the Lord, but I knew under me was death and hell. Satan had targeted me from that accident August 19, 2004, when a truck hit me as I walked across the street. Satan tried to kill me he was not going to let me go. It was like Satan had to get God's permission to afflict Job. I didn't think of the testing Job went through until later but I remembered what Job said. ***Job 13: 15 Though he slay me yet will I trust him: but I will maintain mine own ways before him.***

The most overwhelming of all the experiences I went through was the alarming feel of my face flat on the hood of that truck and my body hanging on the hood of that big black truck and I helplessly sliding down off the hood unto the concrete street, and ending in a sitting position in the street. It was close to a year before I could get that terrifying experience out of my mind. I am sure that had a lot to do with my insomnia, when I close my eyes I saw the hood of that big black truck and me on it.

I asked the Lord what did I do to offend Him I try to show my love for you Lord by living according to your word where did I stray from you?. What ever I did please forgive me. I ask Him to let me know what I did so I would never do it again. I searched my mind to find where my failure was to live for the Lord.

I could not move so I stayed completely still not moving to the right nor to the left. Every part of my body pained. I did not know where the Lord was but I made up in my mind I could do nothing but call upon his name JESUS. I said nothing but JESUS for two weeks or more. When I had to get up I said the name of JESUS for strength. Not only was my body attacked my mind was also, I had dreams that were so real I actually thought I was doing these things.

I was told by some people I did not know that I had a young child overseas, I was a mother. I went overseas with these people to take care of this child that was calling me mother. I believed I was this child's mother I was trying to get this child on a train to come to the United States to care for this child. I did not want to live out of the States. They convinced me that was my child, but I didn't remember having the child or had no idea who the child's father was. I knew I had three children by my husband and they were grown. It was so real I was frightened that I was loosing my mind, I had times of being disoriented I didn't know where I was. At times I was confronted by people I did not know accusing me of things I did not do, and it was so real I thought I was out of my mind. I asked the Lord to protect my mind so I would not loose it. ***2 Timothy 1: 7 For God hath not given us the spirit of fear; but of power, and of love, and of a sound mine.***

This Little Light Of Mine

I went to the hospitals by ambulance I was given a MRI the results were I was told I had a fractured tailbone with bruised muscles internally, a pelvis that moved up injuring the back muscles. My entire body went out of biologically control. There are things the body can do to torment you like itch in hands, itch in feet and toes, where you can't scratch to get relief, that agony lingered and endured for weeks to buff me. The suffering from carpal tunnel in the left hand caused severe pain and extra torment to me. In addition my Diabetes flared up my blood sugar dropped too low and made me very sick. When I checked my blood sugar It would also get very high it seemed to take a while to get it under controlled. My blood sugars rose and dropped like a roller coaster daily to keep me sick internally. I lost my appetite and had to force myself to eat that was a new experience and not a pleasant one, while waiting weeks for my body to adjust to several Insulin changes my doctor trying to get the right dosage to get my sugar under control. I was very sick during this time and thought I would die. I lost 28 pounds..

Trying to be obedient to the doctor and dietitian I had to eat measured amounts of every thing. I had to eat 4 snacks with three meals a day.
All these illness collectively at once were pounding my mind, soul, and body. It was too much to bear but this scripture came to mind. *1 Corinthians 13: There hath no temptation taken you but such as is common to man: but God is faithful who will not suffer you to be tempted above that ye are able: but with the temptation also make a way to escape: that ye maybe able to bear it.* The Lord knows how much you can bear. Going through this sickness I had to go over my life searching to find out what sin did I commit or did I disobey the Lord? what did I do to deserve what is happing to me?. I know I was glad when He lifted some of this torment off me. I still felt like I was walking dead moving in terrible pain. I was given medication to help me sleep this was a first in my life I had to have something to sleep but I only took one. The one I took made me dizzy and sick. I was also given medication for depression but I did not take them. I never took them before I was always afraid it would affect my mind so I would never take them. After some time I was able to sleep for a few hours and that was a breakthrough for me. To sleep with out fear of the recurrent pain, fear of the dreams that startled me and would awake me if I dozed off. A real fear of not waking up lasted a long time and still remains with me, to the point I am so great full when I do awake I give God the praise for His Grace and Mercies to let me wake to see another day.

When I began to sleep a little better I felt so much better in my body I felt as if I might live thru this. There were nights I tried to sleep, but it was interrupted not only by pain but thoughts came in my mind that woke me up startled. In my book I remember a chapter I wrote entitled Trust Him when you cannot Trace Him, again I had to recall this truth. During this time of trial and testing the Spirit and the Word tells me the Lord is with me and would never leave me nor forsake me even though I can't Trace Him. I had to Trust Him. I put my faith in overdrive again and trust Him to bring me out.

I kept telling my self this soon will pass it will soon be over don't give up. I went through my mind searching what have I done to get in this condition ? the Lord will bring me through. I kept saying the name of JESUS, JESUS was my Lord and He alone will I serve. I knew in whom I believed and He was able to bring me through I believed the scripture that tells me 1 *John 4: 4 Greater is he that is in you then he that is in the world.*

I knew I served a God that healed my body when I had a withered arm His name is Jesus. In the scriptures *Isaiah 54: 17 No weapon that is formed against thee shall prosper; and every tongue that shall arise against thee in judgment thou shall condemn. This is the heritage of the servants of the Lord, and their righteousness is of me, saith the Lord.*

My body was finally beginning to get adjusted to the change of medication and I began to feel better. I tell you what a relief it was not having that sick feeling I had endured so long from Satan buffing me, I find my self thanking and praising the Lord for the little relief he gave me as well as the increase relief he gives me every day from this illness. My heart is grateful for how the Lord is delivering me out of this illness. I am not completely healed I still have severe pain in my back if I stand or walk to much but I am praising the Lord in advance for complete healing. In His word He tells me by His stripes I am healed. *Isaiah 53: 5 But he was wounded for our transgressions he was bruised for our iniquities: the chastisement of our peace was upon him and with his stripes we are healed.*

Oh the shock I felt when I received the news my sister in law died suddenly. She had not been ill, but fell dead raking leaves in her yard. We talked to each other every evening she had a triple bypass several years ago. I realized we are here today and gone tomorrow. We know not when we will leave this earth. The Lord knows when He will call each one of us. I had expected I would have gone before her because I was that sick. She and my brother were so busy going all the time active for the Lord. I could not see how I would make it to her funeral I asked one of my cousins if I could go with her family

This Little Light Of Mine

to the funeral she told me she didn't want three people riding in the back seat I could not go.

I wanted my granddaughter to go with me. I didn't feel well enough to drive, I doubt weather my car would have make it. I want to tell the world God will work all things out for you if you put it in his hands. He worked it out. I called another cousin of mine to notify her of my sister-in-law's death, a few days later she and her husband decided they would go and asked me and my granddaughter to go with them if I wanted too. I was so glad the Lord worked it out for my granddaughter and I to go, he provided the money. and gave me a touch in my body that I felt well enough to make the trip with some pain and discomfort. The Lord sent my granddaughter and I to Ohio in luxury we were totally impressed and far greater then what we could have dreamed of. What A mighty God I serve. Thank you Lord.

The doctor suggested Physical Therapy for the pain in my back. Because the accident cause my pelvis to move up causing slight injury to my back muscles. I went to therapy two times a week for weeks. The pain from the Physical Therapy became unbearable I told the Lord I was not going to Physical Therapy but I was stretching out on faith Trusting him to heal me.

My granddaughter who loves her grandmother dearly paid for a Cruise to Nassau for my birthday as a surprise. I was too sick to go. I tried to get booking for her so she could go to help me. The air fare price went up so high we couldn't afford it, she lost the money she paid in full. I appreciated the thought and I love her very much for trying to surprise me for my birthday. I thank God for her and how she helps me daily I love her dearly and thank God for her. I pray I will be able to take her on a Cruise one day.

Weeks later I was able to stand and walk a few more steps than before with less pain in my back, the Lord reduced the severe pain. I felt discomfort from a great deal of tension moving from the lower back muscles up to my shoulders and neck, causing dull pain and ache I found out I was having muscle spasms. With a new medication I began to feel better. Sleeping good at night helped me very much. I felt well enough to return to my Bible study, and Prayer Warriors. I know the Lord was healing me and will continue to pour his healing on me everyday. The pain is felt in my back after a long time. My pain extends down my buttocks. I will praise him I will glorify him, magnify Him I will tell of his Grace and Mercies to deliver me from the hands of the devil and from death.

James 5: 26 15-16 And the prayer of faith shall save the sick, and the

Lord shall raise them up: and if he have committed any sins, they shall be forgiven him. The Lord impressed upon me to give an alter call to any one that has read my Testimony of how the Lord has raised me up from the portals of hell the devil wanted to put me in. I held the Lord high and lifted up in my life and I will in my death and to him I give all the glory and praise.

I would like for you to see the value of turning your life over to the Lord now and not to wait any longer for now is the day of Salvation. Do not wait until you get sick to turn your life over to the Lord, do it while you are well. Make sure You mean it from your heart. The Lord reads your heart he will know if you mean it. You will go through temptation, trials and testing from Satan and you need to have God on your side to see you through. You must make up your mind to seek him, except him, and live for him if you wait it might be too late The word says today is the day of Salvation tomorrow is not promised. ***1John 4:10 Herein is love, not that we loved God, but that he loved us, and gave his Son to be propitiation for our sins. Whosoever believeth in the Lord Jesus Christ shall be saved.*** Except his love now and began to watch him give you a new life, peace, joy and happiness. You too can say with me my soul loves and magnifies the Lord.

I thank the Lord God for resurrecting me by His Grace and Mercies.

Luke 23: 43 And there appeared an Angel unto him from heaven, strengthening him

Chapter 4

BEWARE OF WHO ANGELS ARE

This was such a lovely day and at my granddaughter's suggestion we prepared to go shopping. I want you to know the Lord is healing me after being hit by a truck walking across the street going into the Beauty Shop I had gone to for about two years, before going to work one day. I was taken to the hospital via ambulance and given a MRI which disclosed I had a fractured tail bone, back muscle strain, a bulge on a disk, and two pinch nerves on both sides of my back. I have been in bed for a long period of time in great back pain, and I was trying to get up and about a little more. My granddaughter had been taking care of me and she does not drive I knew she would like to get out so I took my pain medicine and started to let her have a breather for she was so faithful in helping me to get around also with the help of the Lord.

We arrived at the store and I noticed a police car parked where I usually park. I parked in the front parking space two spaces down from the police car. I looked and saw the windows were dark but it looked like someone was in the police car. I told my granddaughter to go on in the store I would wait for her in the car, I didn't think I would be able to walk around in the store with her to shop. I sat in my car for a while to get strength to get out of the car I decided to walk a little since I had only walked around in the house. I got out of my car with great difficulty and sever pain I walked in front of my car and down to several cars with so much pain but making an effort to walk. I was so glad I was able to put my weight on my two feet I was walking with my cane, for I really needed it for the effort to walk was painful. I thought I was better than I really was. I was bent over trying to get to my car as fast as I could to sit down. On the way to my car I gave a nod to the police like good afternoon when a policewomen stepped out of the car. Coming toward me she said "I see you are having a problem walking can I help you"?. I stopped dead in my tracks number one it was not a policeman but a police woman number two she asked me if she could help me. I said thank you for asking but my car is right here. She asked me what happened to me, you walk as if you are in so much pain. I watched you get out of your car and walking, you seemed to be in great pain. I told her I had been hit by a truck a couple weeks ago walking to the beauty shop and taken to the hospital. I was given a MRI the findings were a suffered a fractured tailbone, and back problem due to the accident and I was in great pain, and I was thankful to be alive. If it had not been for the Lord the lady that hit me could have been going faster and knocked me down and ran over me. She was on a cell phone and said " I didn't see you, I didn't see you, I didn't see you.

She asked me to come closer to her car and I did, people were walking all around us going into the store I am sure they were wondering what has she done to have a police talking to me. The onlookers didn't seem to bother her, she was doing what the Lord told her to do. She opened the back door I was totally unprepared for what came next, she took out a bottle of blessed oil. I was shocked, at that time my granddaughter walked up, the policewoman began to pray for me anointing me with the oil. I could feel the power of the Holy Ghost fall on all of us. When she finished praying we were unable to move we began to praise the Lord. The entire area was covered with a cloud of glory and angels. She put the bottle of oil back in the backseat of the car and my granddaughter saw her Bible in the back seat.

I never thought I would ever see a policeman or police woman carrying Blessed Oil and a Bible in the back of their police car and would pray for me. The Lord reminded me and said He has angels and prayer warriors everywhere and in all kinds of uniforms. She and I both were touched by the Sprit of the Lord that day, I often include her in my prayer and I know she prays for me. She was helpful in my healing also in getting a report of the accident for me. She was working in the store my daughter went into as a store Detective. She is a born again Christian and very active in her church. An angel used by God to minister to me His servant thank you Jesus. ***Hebrews 13: 2 Let Brotherly love continue. Be not forgetful to entertain strangers: thereby some have entertained angels unawares.***
I was impressed like me she was not shy or bothered by the people that were watching her or listening to her she was about her fathers business. I was not ashamed to have her anoint me and pray for me. ***Romans 1:16 For I am not***

This Little Light Of Mine

ashamed of the gospel of Christ: for it is the power of God unto salvation to ever one that believeth: to the Jew first, and also to the Greek.

The Lord Jesus Christ is so good he sends people to us to do whatever he has for us to do or to carry out what ever he wants us to say or do. I think of many times the Lord would anoint me to speak to people I didn't know and never seen before. As I was reflecting back I am reminded of the day the Lord put a Catholic Nun right in my lap, that's right in direct contact with me.

I was working at my job as a nurse in a hospital when a Nun appeared on my floor at the hospital. She approached me as if she knew me for many years, I was shocked at how the Lord let this Nun attached herself to me until the Lord said this is the end. It began with a conversation about the Lord and every conversation we had from the first day was about the Lord Jesus and his word. The Lord would give the anointing, the scriptures, and allow me to witness to her. I remember how hungry she was for the word of God. *2 Timothy 2: 24: And the servant of the Lord must not strive: but be gentle unto all men, apt to teach, patient, In meekness instructing those that oppose themselves; if God peradventure will give them repentance to the acknowledging of the truth:*

I do not remember the scriptures I was giving to her from the Lord: at lunch time, on breaks, and anytime we could read the Bible or discuss the scripture and it was remarkable how she remembered the scriptures she was given. The Lord was bringing her closer to Him in order for her to understand the scriptures and to receive Salvation, the Holy Ghost and to be Baptized in water. The only time she was not with me was when I went home. When I came on the floor she met me there, when the Lord assign someone to you, you will complete the mission to the end. When you have accomplished everything he wants you to accomplish with that person He will take them away as quickly as he put them in your life. This is exactly what he did. *1 Timothy: 16 All Scripture is given by inspiration of God, and is profitable for doctrine, of reproof, for correction, for instruction in righteousness.*

He allowed me to hear her testimony before her time was up. It was several weeks before I saw her again. She met me one day in the morning and said "I have received Salvation from my Lord and Saviour Jesus Christ and the Baptism of the Holy Ghost". " I have been giving the other Nuns that live in the convent with me the scriptures, teachings and they have received Salvation, the Baptism of the Holy Ghost also, we will be Baptized in water."

21

Emerged or buried in water. We are thankful he appointed you to lead us to except him and be saved, and turned us to the Light as He is the Light.

When she told me her testimony the Holy Ghost fell on us and we rejoiced unashamed of who we loved the Lord Jesus. We were praising Him and giving Him the glory. What a blessing to have witness salvation to the Catholic nun and lead her to Christ as the Lord anointed me to do. ***Luke 14: 23 And the Lord said unto the servant, Go out into the highways and hedges, and compel them to come in, that my house may be filled.***

Amen and Amen to the will of God.

Romans 3: 23-24. For all have sinned and come short of the Glory of God; being justified freely by his grace through the redemption that is in Christ Jesus:

Chapter 5

NOTHING BUT THE GRACE OF GOD

Have you ever had a day that you feel as if nothing could happen to you that was not good and the best is the only thing that could come your way? I was feeling good with not a pain any where in my body. I was going to the Beauty Shop to get my hair done then I was going to work looking good. I parked my car as I usually do across the street on a school lot, because the beauty shop lot was too full with not much room to park and get out. The light turned and stopped the traffic so I hurried across the street walking when a big black truck coming out of the parking lot came right into my left side. I was face down on the hood the truck lifted me up and dropped me down into the street on my behind. The lady in the truck was on a cell phone and said she didn't see me, she kept repeating she didn't see me she never put down the cell phone nor did she get out of the truck.

I set in the street until the Ambulance came the traffic was held up and cars backed up. A man driver of the first car got out of is car and held my hand until the Ambulance came. I relied on my beautician to get his name and phone number along with other witness but she never did. I could not do anything but thank the Lord I was alive. The truck was not going too fast. had she been going a little faster she would have knocked me down and ran over me. I was wondering why a police did not come and ask me questions I saw one talking to the lady who was driving the truck for a long time. I wondered why a police didn't put a blanket over me I was sitting in my white pants in the street thank God I was dressed for work and I work in pants. The entire time I was sitting in the street I was praying and saying the name of Jesus. I was thanking him for not letting the devil kill me, and asking him to help me. I asked my beautician to call my job to let them know what happened, she was there but stayed a distance from me. Later I found out she never called my job to let them know what happened to me in fact I never heard from her for a year later. A year latter I found out my beautician was friends with the lady. The lady that hit me was a booster and sold clothes in the beauty shop. I make sure I pray for all the people involved in that accident.

I was taken to Wishard Hospital and treated for pain, and shock. I was given Morphine and taken for a MRI. The MRI showed I had a Fractured Tailbone medically called a fractured Coccyx's. The Doctor told me there was nothing they could do for that kind of fracture but give me pain medication to keep me comfortable. I was given medication that just was not strong enough to take the pain away. I was released from the hospital. I suffered with that pain for two years and a half and was not compensated for the injury. I can not tell you the extent of the pain I have suffered as the results from the woman that hit me was talking on a cell phone up to her ear, kept saying to me over and over " I am sorry I didn't see you". She never got off the phone or got down out of that big black truck to see about me. I was stretched out on top of her hood and she hit a curb and I fell off the hood onto the street. The woman that was driving the truck did not have insurance her insurance had been terminated six months before she ran into me. I have not been able to understand this injustices. I have to pay my insurance coverage every month. I try to do what the law says.

At the time I am writing this I am not out of the woods yet but my Faith has just gone into overdrive again and I see a little more light. I do not know what the title of this miracle Chapter will be, the Lord has not given it to me yet. When He does it will exceed any awesome experiences you have had or can conceive. He has not bought me out of this terrible pain completely yet, but I am still rocking on unsteady legs and footing waiting for more of his strength to overpower me. I am willing to testified to others what the Lord is bringing me through. I can say I would not want any one to go through these experiences. I can't wait to give these experiences to you. Hold on as I am holding on to Him the Author and Finisher of my faith. I need His GRACE and MERCY to help me through.

I thought the Lord was going to let Satan have me when I let go, I am speaking of the tortuous weeks going into months, I could not sleep for the picture of that big truck in my eyes as I was on top of the hood and the pain I had in my back. This was a life threatening time for Satan was out to end my life but I kept saying the name of Jesus, the most important name I knew, and the Lord kept me He held me up and lifted me up and out, He did not let me go. Glory Halleluiah.

Every day it is a challenge to stand, or take two steps to walk without sever pain in my back. I thought I would have to get around in a wheelchair. I am fighting as hard as I can to keep from becoming wheel chair dependent. The doctor prescribes medication for the pain but it does not take the pain away completely. I am reluctant about taking the added amount that he gives me PRN that it might take the pain away. I have a high tolerance to pain, but I suffer a great deal of pain. I try to prevent taking pain medication in the large amounts or dosage. It is easier for me to drive and sit in the car while my granddaughter goes in the store for I cannot walk around without pain in my back. I constantly ask the Lord to heal me of the pain for I am limited in every thing I try to do. I take two pain pills and two muscle relaxes to go to church and I can barely make it from the car into the church. I cannot go any where for the pain is extreme.

I continue praying to the Lord for his healing power to heal me. *Have Mercy upon me, O Lord; for I am weak; O Lord, heal me for my bones are vexed. Psalms 6:2 But he was wounded for our transgression was bruised for our iniquities: the chastisement of our peace was upon him; and with his stripes we are healed. Isaiah 53:5.*

I had the desire to resume my meeting with the Prayer Warriors of my church I made an effort to be present at the next meeting, I was in so much pain I could not attend. I could see myself slowly going downhill becoming dependent on someone (my Granddaughter) to help me and being wheelchair bound. Attending church was also a strong desire I had. I never neglected going to church nothing ever stopped me. I Thank God for giving me the strength to attend and providing a parking spot close to the church door, so I didn't have too far to walk He has been faithful to do that.

If you have been fortunate not to have a bad back with severe pain then you have no idea what pain you will experience. The pain cause me to become immobile I had to sit most of the time in order to be free of the pain. Whatever I tried to do I would be in pain I feel like someone else was in my body, I feel older then my age, I am stripped of my independence, and not being able to stand long, walk far, or move without pain in my back, I could see working any more is out of the question.

This condition with my back has continued for over two years. I never gave up hope that the Lord would heal my back in his due time and in his way. The Lord has worked miracles in my life many times before he has healed me and I know he will again. I had been going to a pain doctor since the accident, he told me he could give me three injections to help me. I have considered the first injection because the pain persist and seemed to move up to the neck and back of neck into the shoulder. I still have the faith the Lord will heal me in His due time. The pain goes down to the buttocks now one buttock and then the other.

It is my high Holy Week the week of the Crucifixion of Christ and I tell you I have had less pain and discomfort, along with the terrible sick feeling that accompanies the pain. I am leaning on the Scripture I previously quoted from *Isaiah 53: 5 But he was wounded for our transgression, he was bruised for our iniquities: the chastisement of our peace was upon him; and with his stripes we are healed.*
I believe he will restore my health back to me, I feel I am slowly getting back up on my feet. I am holding my head higher, my eyes seam to be open wider, and I am talking louder, and I will continually praise his holy name, he is my God and I am loved by him. Earlier in another Chapter of my book I ask God the question what did I do to be chastised with this pain? I could not remember anything I have done since the Lord restored me years ago to deserve this pain. I asked the Lord to forgive me what ever I had done, and whatever sin I had committed. I prayed as Job prayed. *Job 6:23 Deliver me from the enemy's hand? or Redeem me from the hand of the mighty? Teach me, and I will hold my tongue and cause me to understand wherein I have erred.*

When I was reminded of how the Lord suffered persecution I was sadden for our Lord did suffer and died for our sins and he was with out sin. Thank you Lord. He arose the third day and ascended into heaven for our sins. The pain continued and I went to a pain specialist he explained to me as the results of the accident of the truck hitting me, and at my age my body has been thrown me into Arthritis he prescribed medication for that. I took the medication and it helped the pain in my neck. after I took it for several months. As the days passed I began to feel less pain in my neck. I could not believe I was beginning to be free of that severe pain but It felt less then it was. I am asking the Lord to continue his Revelation knowledge of why I was going through this pain and affliction to my body as long as I have. His word tells me our time is not Gods time. I will continue giving God the glory for what He has done and for what He is doing and what He is going to do for me. At this time I want to thank the Lord for my dear granddaughter the Lord blessed me with, Her name is Kisha and if it had not been for her helping in all needed ways, when you can't do for your self. Responsibility of the house was also placed upon her. I thank her for all she does for me and I thank the Lord for her. My faith is built on nothing else then Jesus blood and righteousness I dare not trust the sweetest frame but wholly lean on Jesus name.

Matthew 25: 39- 40
Or when saw we thee sick, or in prison, and came unto
thee? And the King shall answer and say unto them. Verily
I say unto you in as much as ye have done it unto the
least of these my brother, ye have done it unto me.

Chapter 6

GOD CAN DO ANY THING

Do you want to know what made it a good day, I will tell you. I woke up breathing, jumped up to the shower and began to thank God for his goodness to wake me up on this side of heaven. I also thank him for allowing me to see the sun shine so bright to bring to my mind how great thou art. I was off from work today an could go back to bed if I wanted to, or go out to the Mall and take a look at the new clothes in the stores. It was that kind of day I could do anything I wanted to do.

As I was drying off from the shower when the phone rang, I was not going to work this day no matter who didn't show up for work. I was off and I am going to do something I want to do this day. I answered the phone Hello and heard my cousin Susie who lived in the Bronx she was crying hysterically. I asked why are you crying she told me the FBI have just arrested Michael her son. I ask what happened, she asked me if I would come to the Bronx and pick her up and she would tell me all about it. I told her I was on the way. I dressed and I was on the way to a very unexpected experiential day.

It is quit a long distance from Jamaica Queens across the Throgs Neck Bridge to the Bronx. I took advantage of the time to pray the whole time I was driving. I had never heard my cousin Susie in such a state as she was but I could understand it was her son. A son who attended a Academy for special smart children, and he made straight A's. He was never in any trouble he was only 15 years old. I prayed the Lord would be with Susie to give her strength

This Little Light Of Mine

to go through this. Still praying I was nearing the White Plans exit, soon I would be at Buckner Blvd. than her apartment.

She got into the car and told me her son robbed three banks one after the other on a bicycle and on foot. He has been arrested and taken down town Manhattan to a prison called the Tombs. Susie was crying and shacking she was a nervous wreck. I told her Susie it is time for us to get direction from the Lord. I stopped the car and we prayed I didn't know what else to do but to pray. I did not have a clue what to about prisons or court procedures, I had never had to face this situation before. God said in his word he would be with me *Joshua 1: 5 As I was with Moses, so I will be with thee: I will not fail thee, nor forsake thee.* I told her we will go and get Michael out and you can take him home. I had to think that way if I thought of what I was saying I would chock.

The jail I am speaking of is about 18 stories high or maybe more to the sky. It is a dark gloomy building police going all over the place. We walked up to the Information desk and I told the officer we were there to get Michael out. After I said that I stepped back and started to shake the thought came to me you must be out of your mind to think you can come in here and take him out of here. This is a prison and you are dealing with the FBI. The reality shook me and I cringed. We were asked to take a seat, after waiting a short while we were led into a office and told to have a seat the door was shut. Soon the door opened and Michael with two FBI officers came into the room. Michael was not handcuffed but sat at a table with the officers. One of the officers asked who was the mother Susie answered she was, I told them I was his cousin and he didn't belong here, and he made a mistake robbing those Banks. He was not the kind of person that would do this. He was a quite person and had respect for people. He was an intelligent young man and an excellent student in school he has no correctional problems.

His mother handed all the school records of Michael's from day one and the officers were impressed, after specking in private with each other they responded with we are puzzled why a young man of his character would want to rob three Banks one after the other, the same morning, in the same area, with no gun or weapon of any kind riding a bicycle and returning all the money to the Bank. When we questioned him he said he did not know why he did such a thing other than he wanted to see if he could do it. We are going to release him to you we believe you are a Christian women but he will have to be released by a Judge. They said to me we will want him to see a Psychiatrist at the Bronx Hospital. They took us to a Judge who talked to Michael for some time and dismissed

29

the case. I talked to the FBI men and reassured them nothing like this will happen again and you know he has never as much as got a traffic ticket since.

Before I left I prayed with the FBI officers and the Judge thanking them and thanking God for moving in Michaels behalf. We left with Michael in the car and drove to the Bronx Hospital for evaluation. Susie was so happy to have her son out of the FBI hands, she tells everyone I went in that terrible place and got her son out of the FBI's hands. I tell her "Susie it was not me, but the Christ that is in me." It was the Lord that opened those prison doors and released Michael.

I said to her don't you see the Lord in this? He opened those doors of this great prison freeing Michael allowing him to except the Lord for guidance and to receive Psychiatric care if he needed it. I have to remind Susie that I was just the body used by the Lord at that time for that situation. I prayed with Michael and he excepted the Lord as his Savior and my cousin Susie also, she was of Catholic Faith, but excepted Christ as her Lord and Savior.

The Spirit of the Lord God is upon me, because the Lord hath anointed me to preach good tidings unto the meek: he hath sent me to bind up the broken hearted, to proclaim liberty to the captive, and the opening of the prison to them that are bound. Isaiah 61:1

We arrived at the hospital and asked for the psychiatrist after some time he arrived and ask us if Michael was under arrest and asked why he was not accompanied by officers. I explained to the doctor they realized he was not a criminal, but a smart young man who has a great future ahead of him. The Judge released him to me and we are here to see if he needed your help. The Doctor told us he would be admitted into the hospital and given a series of test for a few days. He was concerned where he was to go when discharged from the hospital. I am so glad I had the Judge put in writing to release him to go back home to his mother and back to school as before. The decision was very clear for the doctor after receiving a copy of that paper.

Michael remained in the hospital a few days he contacted an ear infection that was taken care of while there. He was released to go home with his mother, then back to school. The school never knew of the arrest or the disposition. Michael never missed another day of school and made up the work for the days he missed. He graduated from the school in N.Y. making the Deans list.

He enrolled in the University of Arizona after four years he graduated Cum de Laude as an Engineer.

He lived in Arizona for a few years, then later got a job as a engineer in N.Y. and have made major repairs on bridges in N.Y. He is married to his college girl friend and has two sons. He has not been in any trouble of any kind since. Susie his mother my cousin is doing well enjoying her two sons, two grandsons and three granddaughters She never forgets the experience we had while watching our great master work out. Our testimony is Our God Can Do Anything.

Therefore being Justified by Faith we have peace with God through our Lord Jesus Christ, by whom also we have access by faith into grace wherein we stand, and rejoice in hope of the glory of God. Romans:5:2.

Revelation 20: 9 And they went up on the breath of the earth, and compassed the camp of the saints about, and the beloveth city; and fire came down from God out of heaven; and devoured them.

Chapter 7

Is The Beauty Within Or Without?

When I reflect upon my young life here in this city I can't help but think what a change has been made. My father always had a car and we traveled. He liked to go places and always wanted his family with him, but I was always glad to return home. My city was smaller, but it was a good place to live. It had everything we needed. My life was so wonderful as a child. I had the love of a mother and father, and my brothers. We were not rich but we had more than many, we had love for people, love of each one in our family and love for God. We were never hungry my father gave people in our neighborhood food to eat he was a go-get-er and would make things happen for him. We were never cold in the winter months, we always had clothes and shoes. He was there with his truck when large grocery stores would discard food they would deem not fresh, on the second day, my mom would pull back the brown leaves and we ate well.

My father raised chickens, ducks, pigs, and goats right in our back yard. We had a big garden on the side of our house. My dad had good friends one was the father of the famous John Dillinger. My dad would take us in the car out to the Dillingers farm on Sunday and we would wait for him to finish talking to Mr. Dillinger. He knew a lot of people in this city. If he was late getting to the bank and it was closed he is the only person I knew that could get the guard to open it for him to transact his business.

My city was full of love, (for the most part), and I never felt anything but love. My father taught us to love each other and to love others white and black. People had more love for their own people then they do now. Killings were on

This Little Light Of Mine

the downside, Afro Americans killing each other was unheard or very rare. If someone killed another it was big news all on the front page. People got along together generally. Back then I had to fight kids to go to the library, to the public Library it was before Dr. Martin Luther King.

There was a difference made between black and white people, but there was not as much greed as prevail now. I don't remember having to go to different rest rooms because we were taught to go to the toilet before we left home. I found out later in life that Greed, Politics, and Satanic influences is what causes people to show difference to each other. I cannot leave out their non responsive love for God. There were black owned established businesses, owned by men of integrity, educated men, we had a black lawyer that ran for President of the United States. Afro American people had stores, Hotels, Real Estate Companies, Drug stores, Physicians, Dentist, Musicians, Hardware stores, Hotels, Restaurants, Apartment Buildings, Bowling Alleys, Lavish Night Clubs with white and black patrons, Repair shops of all kinds service stations, all kind of services. Now they are not allowed to have any business. People that are foreigners have come into this Country and the State and are allowed to own business, but not blacks. Afro American men were allowed to work on the Sanitation Department, Fire, Police, Ambulance, Highway Department, and Construction Companies. At this time most of these jobs have no or minimal Afro American men working in these capacities. Afro Americans are not able to get these jobs because of discrimination and white monopoly. Afro Americans can not own anything here now. Prices are raised so high Afro Americans can not afford to venture into any thing but churches, mortuaries, beauty shops, etc. This has a lot to do with the color of their skins this is the conditions to this day. Christ said he made us all according to His likeness, and he said He died for us all.

Hold on, don't get too excited! Discrimination existed and has for many years but is in the fore front. We had our babies in a big General Hospital that had a segregated East side of the ward for blacks, and West side for whites. We went to an all black schools, because we were not allowed to go to white schools. We attended an all black High school, the only one in the city. We made our black High school the best in the State at doing almost anything, including basketball and football championships. We excelled in everything we did. We had educated teachers who were intent on teaching us to excel. We had prayer in our school, we respected our parents, our teachers, our church, and elders.

Hate and discrimination was subtle at that time and a shameful thing. Now it is on the surface no longer hidden. There is a spirit of hatred that hovers over this city and the world like a cloud, hatred for people with dark skin people, hatred for the poor people, hatred for Christians, hatred for the Jewish people, hatred for God and his son Jesus Christ. Pick up your morning paper you will read that someone has been killed, drugs, greed and hatred is the main perspective along with many other things mainly satanic control.

Galatians 5: 19-21 The works of the flesh are adultery fornication, uncleanness, lasciviousness, idolatry, witchcraft, hatred, variance, emulation's, wrath, strife, sedition's, heresies, envying, murders, drunkenness, reveling, and they that do such things shall not inherit the kingdom of God. Even the angels followed pernicious ways and covetousness.

2 Peter 2: 4-5 For if God spared not the angels that sinned, but cast them down to hell, and delivered them into chains of darkness, to be reserved unto Judgment. How will we be spared?

And spared not the old world, but saved Noah the eight persons a preacher of rightousness, bringing in the flood upon the world of the ungodly;

"The beauty without" seems to be the criteria now. Men tearing down buildings to rebuild, larger, taller, more beautiful buildings. Buildings that are cheaply built(substandard). We must work to restore "the beauty within" this starts in the heart, love to others, to our city, our world, beginning within ourselves. Hate on the job, within our Federal, State, City and Municipal Departments. Hatred of the word of God, that keeps prayer out of our schools and our country. Hatred in the family, within our homes, parents teaching their children to hate. Hate organizations. Our churches are not coming together as all God's children should. We must stop this spirit of hate that covers our cities, states, and countries and us. It is not of God, but the beginning is within ourselves. We must have love.

1 John 4: 15,20 God is Love. He that dwelleth in love dwelleth in God and God dwelleth in him. He that loveth not his brother whom he sees, how can he love God whom he has not seen?.
If you are bound by any one of these works of the flesh, don't you want to have beauty within? God gave His only begotten Son to free you. He did it through Love. Believe on the Lord Jesus Christ and thou shalt be saved

and thou house. Acts 16: 34. He that believeth and is baptized shall be saved; but he that believeth not shall be damned. Mark 16:16.

For ye are the temple of the living God; as God hath said, I will Dwell in them, and Walk in them: and I will be their God, and they shall be my people. Wherefore come out from among them, and be ye separate, saith the Lord, and touch not the unclean thing; and I will receive you, and I will be a Father unto you, and ye shall be My sons and daughters, saith the Lord Almighty. 2 Corinthians 6: 16-17-18.

1 Corinthians 15: 58 Therefore, my beloved brethren, be ye steadfast, unmovable, always abounding in the work of the Lord, forasmuch as ye know that you labor is not in vain in the Lord.

Chapter 8

WHEN HE OPENS THE DOOR

As I opened my eyes and stepped onto the floor I thanked the Lord for another beautiful day and invited him to be with me the entire day that I may praise him and make this day glorious to him for his goodness to me. Then I was brought down to the reality; The Lord told me to go to the bank and open an account with the little money you have. The bank close to where you live so it will be more convenient That's right I had a small amount to deposit but I am obedient to the Lord. I was a new author and it took the money. I had to put aside money to reorder my books it cost more to reorder books than to publish them.

I was feeling so good as I parked at the bank and went in. I got in line for it seemed I got there at a busy time. A lady who worked in the bank as assistant manager walked up to me and spoke I found my self telling her I was a new author and she asked me the name of my book, I told her A Miracle, Your Obedience, My Testimony. She asked me how could she get one of my books, I was so surprised I said I have some out in my car and I will get you one. I went so fast to the car and got several, two hardback and a soft back. I bought it and handed it to her she said I will take it. Another lady in the line looked as if she was an attorney or teacher said out loud I want one too and she bought one.

Now I guess you would say I had a good productive morning but that's not all. The lady that walked up to me first took care of me and told me come over here to her office she was one of the banks managers. She lead me to her desk and asked me to sit down. She explained to me how I could have a

This Little Light Of Mine

book signing for a month there in the bank if I opened a business account. I asked her where did she say I could have the book signing? she replied here at the bank, I know my mouth flue opened in shock. Well need I tell you I hurried and signed to open that business account. I thanked her for being in position for the Lord to use her to bless me like this. I also thanked the Lord for opening this door to be a blessing to me. Having a book signing at this bank would give me a great deal of exposure for my book the Lord anointed me to write. I was so excited I couldn't wait to tell my granddaughter the good news. At this time I was dealing with some health problems Anemia, no energy, and low blood.

At this time I had just returned home after a week in the Hospital For weakness due to low blood. My blood count went down to 6.0, Therefore I was given blood transfusions. I prayed and asked the Lord to strengthen me and enable me to have this book signing. When Monday came I was feeling better and had my books packed along with all my beautiful table set up I was ready to meet the public, and the public to meet my book.

As soon as the bank was opened my granddaughter, myself and the luggage rolled right in. We began to decorate the table with the white tablecloth with red gathered cloth that went around the table and hung down to the floor. The books were placed on the table in order along with the order sheets, a cute floral arrangement that sat the table off, it drew attention to the cover of the books. The book cover was red, black and a little white, very dramatic and eye catching. I am very proud of the books and their cover because the Lord gave me the direct details how he wanted them to look and what he wanted them to say. I was obedient to the smallest detail and wanted the best for the Lord. In my life I try to give the Lord my best, because he gave his best to me that we might have eternal life.

The staff of the bank were impressed how color full and well organized the table looked and they gave us their approval for our effort and good taste. The people that came into the bank stopped at the table and looked at the books after transacting their banking business. I talked to them about the book and answered their questions about the book they were very impressed and did buy the books. I also took the opportunity to say for the Lord There were numerous statements made like "Oh my wife is mad at me but I will buy this book and that will make up because she like to read good books." One of my favorite reflections was from a man who had bought a book a couple days before, came into the bank and in a loud voice announced to me he was sorry he bought my book. He was so loud every one in the bank stopped and looked at him. I was asking the Lord what had I done for this man to dislike my book after getting the attention of every one he said " I can't get any breakfast, lunch, or supper". he said " because my wife walks around the house reading your book not doing anything else and won't put it down. Every one in the bank laughed and we enjoyed his comedy.

It didn't take long before the atmosphere of the bank took upon a duel purpose the atmosphere of reverence and glorifying God and His presence was truly felt in that place. People were asking how could they be saved, how they could get peace, and change their lives for the better. Leading people to Christ is what I love to do best. People were asking for prayer and asking for guidance in their day to day living. People were heavy laden with grief, problems confronting them, and the Lord gave me what to say and what to pray. Problems of all characteristic of human distinctions, fleshly and spiritual.
People left with a new outlook on their situations, a deeper dedication to live according to the word of God or determination to do the will of the Lord in their lives.

It was a time of reflection on my life and how the Lord helped me with various situations. testing, trials, but he bought me through. I was given a stronger determination to be in Gods' will and to let nothing deter me from my walk holy and upright before the Lord. At all times keeping in my forethought one destination eternal life. In all this my love increased for the creation of all people and praises to our God. First and for most outcome of the effort to introduce my book to the people, or the financial blessing, was the one on one interment praying with people with their personal concern, for some the introduction to Jesus Christ, to others a deeper commitment to Jesus and his word. It was not about me, but all about Him.

2nd Corinthians 1:20. For all the promises of God in him
are yea and in him Amen, unto the glory of God by us.

Chapter 9

PROMISES, PROMISES, PROMISES

There is so much in the Bible for us to absorb, in our Christian life of what thus say-eth the Lord. I am not saying you are not right, but what I am saying is we have a tendency to forget such great and important truths in the scriptures as an example of God's Promises. It maybe that we don't believe they are important, or you don't know them, or theirs too many of them, or you remember them only when you hear them mentioned. To a born again Christian they are like a blood transfusion to an Anemic. It is like a life raft to a drowning man. To me I have found it to be a direct life line to my Saviors heart. My mother always told me you can't tell most people anything, a few people a few things, and the remainder nothing. I want to tell you something for you to understand I will tell you in such a simple way with the hope you will hear, receive, and apply the word.

For the last year and a half I have been afflicted with severe pain in my back, gluteus, hips, and neck. I hope you have never had such pain and that you never will have the experience in your lifetime. I read the word daily, prayed and ask the Lord to heal me, I prayed the healing scriptures, and cried them out daily, I prayed the Psalms and cried them out daily, it was when I called out to the Lord his promises to me in his word that I got results along with prayer of the Elders.

I remember this promise " I will never leave you nor forsake you". Do you see I had this pain over two years so long I had to be reminded of this promise, I had to be reminded he knew all about my pain, how severe it was, how long I had it, what it made me do. Oh Lord forgive me for the times I cried out in pain for you to release me from my suffering. At the time I did not think of the pain the Lord suffered on Calvary, Now I know, and see my suffering was to make me a partner of Christ suffering. I could forgive the woman that hit me while talking on a cell phone and said she didn't see me crossing the street. How I would take it when I found out she had no Insurance. Satan tried me to prove how much I loved the Lord Jesus Christ, how sincere I was about my relationship with the Lord. How much I love my fellow man, how I felt about my enemies, how I loved my family including my church family, etc. An attack on me in every area of my life. He was very thorough and persistent. The Lord gave His promise to me. *2 Corinthians 4:17-18 For our light affliction which is but for a moment worketh for us a far more exceedingly and eternal weight of Glory. While we look not at the things which are seen, but at the things which are not seen: for the things which are seen are temporary; but things which are not seen are eternal.*

At this point I would like to let you know what I think of the Devil. I Hate him, I rebuke him, I put his head under my foot and squash him, etc. The best thing I do to him is call on the name of Jesus,. He hates the name of Jesus and I love to say the name of Jesus to him and let him know the resurrection power of God is greater then he is. I send him to the pit where he is from and where he belongs. I let him know the Blood of Jesus is against him and all his evil, and he is defeated by the power of the Lord Jesus Christ. I remind him of the hell he will live in, he and his demons. I remember the Lords word he gave tome. *Behold I give you power to tread upon Serpents and Scorpions and over all the power of the enemy: and nothing shall by any means hurt you. Notwithstanding in this rejoice not, that the sprits are subject unto you; but rather rejoice, because your names are written in heaven. Luke 10: 19-20.*

Before I go any further I would like to share with you some of the promises that helped me:

Unfailing: *1 King 8: 56 Blessed be the Lord that hath given rest unto his people Israel, according to all that he promised; there hath not failed one word of all his good promise, which he promised by the hand of Moses his servant.*

Assured by Devine Ability: *Romans 4: 21 And being fully persuaded that what he had promised he is able also to perform.*

Of Infinite Value: *2 Peter 1-4 Whereby are given to us exceeding great and precious promises; that by these we might be partakers of the divine nature having escaped the corruption that is in the world through lust.*

Brighter days: *Psalms 30: 5 For his anger endured for a moment; In his favor is life: weeping may endure for a moment: but joy cometh in the morning.*

Deliverance: *Psalms 34: 10* Many are the afflictions of the righteous but the Lord delivered him out of them all.

Devine care in sickness: *Psalms 41: 3 Psalms 50: 15 The Lord will strengthen him upon the bed of languishing: thou shall make all his bed in his sickness. (to be in a miserable state of mind)*

Comfort of God's Presence: *Isaiah 14: 3 When thou passeth through the waters I will be with thee: and through the rivers they shall not over flow thee when thou walkest through the fire thou shalt not be burned neither shall the flame kindle upon thee.*

An Eternal home: *John 14*: 1 Let not your heart be troubled : ye believe in God believe also in me. In my fathers house are many mansions: if it were not so, I would have told you. I go to prepare a place for you.

All things work for the believers good: Romans 8:28 And we all know that all things work together for good to them that love God. To them who are the called according to his purpose. 2 Corinthians 4:1 7 for our light afflictions is for a moment worketh for us a far more exceeding and external weight of glory:

Sufficiency of Divine Grace; 2Corinthians 12:9. And he said unto me My Grace is sufficient for thee for my strength is made perfect in weakness. Most gladly therefore will rather glory in my infirmities that the power of Christ may rest upon me.

Fellowship in Christ Suffering: 1Peter 4:12 -13 Beloved think it not strange concerning the fiery trials which is to try you, as though some strange thing happened unto you: But rejoice, inasmuch as ye are partakers of Christ's suffering;

Promises of *life Luke 10: 27- 28*
And he answering said, Thou Shalt love the Lord Thy God with all thy

Heart and with all Thy Soul, And with all Thy Strength, And with All Thy Mind: and Thy Neighbor as Thy self. And he said unto him Thou hast answered right: this do; and thou shalt live.

These are just a few of God's Promises, but many more run through the Bible like ribbons read them and be blessed. Remember to stand on the promises of God. Our daily living is based upon His promises. You can find one to carry you through whatever we are going through. His purpose for all His promises is to encourage us, strengthen us, heal us, comfort us, raise us out of all our troubles, and build up our faith in Him our Lord and Savior Jesus Christ.

*Romans 6: 23 For the wages of sin is death; but the gift of
God is eternal life through Jesus Christ our Lord.
Romans 3: 23 For all have sinned and come short of the Glory of God.*

Chapter 10

SIN AND BEAR ITS RESULTS

The American Heritage Dictionary states Sin: Transgression of a religious or moral law: Something shameful or wrong. What a watered down definition. Sin is one of the oldest acts man has ever committed. The origin stems from the beginning of man when Satan raised his ugly head and caused Adam and Eve to fall from Gods' perfection. To this day sin is prevalent, openly practiced, and is the way of life for most of all humanity. People have a heathenish type of existence, irreligious, unenlightened, uncivilized, and immoral characteristics. As a matter of fact, instead of the practice of sin being the wrong way to go, it seems to be the only way. According to the world's majority, this is the most popular road to take to get where you are going and desire to go.

Life is moving so fast it takes all your day and nights to keep up with the pace of every day living. That is if you are among the post described persons mentioned. I hate to tell you we are fast approaching an eternal fast decent into Hell or Hades. To live in this fast moving cycle of time you do not have time for anything to slow you down; you feel you must stay ahead of the game. You cannot afford to take the time to consider anything that might change your profile or destination. Your goal is to soar above everything to avoid most hindrances to excel and succeed to get ahead of the Jones.

At this time I feel I must stop and give you the correct definition for sin. According to the greatest authority on sin, he who cast the demonic angels from Heaven because they sinned by thinking they were as great and greater than their creator God.

#1 Sin------- To *have any other gods before (Him) Exodus 34:14*
For thou shalt worship no other god: for the Lord, whose name is Jealous is a jealous God.
God said in his word I am a jealous God. In the world we live in, people have put everything before God as their number one priority. Some people do not know God as their Creator and they put other gods before him. An Atheist; ***Psalms 53: 1 A fool hath said in his heart, there is no God. Corrupt are they, and have done abdominal Iniquity, their is none that doeth good.*** They think God is an molten image made of Jade. Some think He is an animal they worship a cow. While they are starving for lack of food they refuse to kill the animal and eat the meat to sustain their lives. Some people give him other names as Mohammad, these names strip him of his Creditability, Deity, Holiness, and Righteousness. ***1 Corinthians 10: 14 Wherefore, my dearly beloved, flee from idolatry.***

People put money before God, they think money is the first thing they need and all they need, They believe if you have money you didn't need anything or anybody else. They believe money will buy whatever you need or want. I would ask you could your money buy one minute of breath if the Lord says it is time for you to meet Him in death?

I agree that money is important its true. We need it, but I believe we need God more, and everything we have he provides. We are told to love God not to love money. ***1 Timothy 6: 10 For the love of money is the root of all evil: which while some coveted after, they have erred from the faith, and pierced themselves through with many sorrows.***
If a rich man had a condition come upon him with severe pain in his body; after consulting a doctor was treated for a while then told by the doctor he has done all he can do for him. The doctor tells him he needs God to work a miracle to save his life. The rich man responds to the doctor "I need whom?". Then he thinks back when he was alone he was reminded of what the old man that takes care of his lawn told him some time ago. Your going to need my God one of these days, you had better seek him now and repent. Learn of him now so he will know you down the road when you need him.

2 sin----- Blaspheming---- against the Holy Ghost and Grieve not the Holy Ghost. This is the only sin you cannot be forgiven of. For other sin Jesus is our advocate to the Father for forgiveness. The Holy Ghost is the third person in the Trinity *Matthew 12: 31-32 Wherefore I say unto you. All manner of sin and blasphemy shall be forgiven unto man; but the blasphemy against*

the Holy Ghost shall not be forgiven unto men. And whosoever speaketh a word against the Son of man, it shall be forgiven unto him: but the blasphemy against the Holy Ghost shall not be forgiven unto men, Neither in the world, neither in the world to come.

Ephesians 4:30 and grieve not the Holy Spirit of God, whereby ye are sealed unto the day of redemption.

3 sin---------Unbelief of no Faith *Romans 14: 23 And he that doubteth is dammed if he eat, because he eateth not of faith: for whatsoever is not of faith is sin.*

Mark9: 23 Jesus said unto them, "If thou canst believe, all things are possible to them that believeth

Romans 10: 17 Faith cometh by hearing and hearing by the word of God.

Revelation 21: 7-8 He that over cometh shall inherit all things; and I will be his God ad he shall be my son, But the fearful, and unbelieving and the abominable, and murderers, and whoremongers, and sorcerers, and idolaters, and all liar, shall have their part in the lake which burneth with fire and brimstone: which is the second death.

St. John 8: 24 I said therefore unto you, that ye shall die in your sins: for if ye believe not that I am He ye shall die in your sins.

If you don't believe the word of God as being the true word a light in our pathway. Leading us into righteousness and holiness that we might have eternal life; you are a dead man walking in a live world. The devil has you dead already when you could be alive and have he joy the Lord gives through Salvation to Eternal Life.

Hebrews 11:1. Now faith is the substance of things hoped for, the evidence of things not seen.
If you don't have faith in God who do you have faith in? No one can perform their promises to us, no one but God. He will and He does. Have faith in God and in His son Jesus Christ.

4 sin---------Pride *Proverbs 16: 18 Pride goeth before destruction, and*

an haughty spirit before a fall. Proverbs 29: 23 A men's pride shall bring him low but honor shall uphold the humble in spirit.

James 4: 6 God resisted the proud, but giveth grace to the humble.
Mark 7: 21- 23 For from within, out of the heart of men proceed evil thoughts, pride, foolishness. All these things come from within and defile the man. Shall we take a look at the results of sin; *Romans 6:23 For the wages of sin is death; but the gift of God is eternal life through Jesus Christ our Lord* Sin always has a response or repercussions that can be rapid or delayed.

5 sin------Foolishness *Proverbs 12: 23 A Prudent man consealeth knowledge but the heart of fools proclaimeth foolishness.*

2Timothy 3:9 But they shall proceed no further for their folly shall be manifest unto all men as theirs also was.

Proverbs 15: 14 The heart of him that hath understanding seeketh knowledge: but the mouth of fools feedeth on foolishness.
Foolishness will cause you to lie, slander, mock sin, despise instructions, meddle, have self-confidence, dishonesty, whoremongers, unclean person, covetous man, and full of hypocrisy.

Ephesians 5: 4 Neither filthiness, nor foolish talking, nor jesting, which are not convenient: but rather giving of thanks.

6 Sin ----- Envy -----
Titus 3: 3, 5, For we ourselves also were sometimes foolish, disobedient, deceived, serving divers lust, and pleasures, living in malice and envy, hateful, and hating one another. Not by works of righteousness, which we have done, but according to his mercy he saved us, by the washing of regeneration, and renewing of the Holy Ghost.

Proverbs 24: 1, 2, Be not envious against evil men, neither desire to be with them. For their hearts studieth destruction and their lips talk of mischief.

7 ----- Lust----*1 John 2: 16, 17, For all that is in the world the lust of the flesh, and the lust of the eyes, and the pride of life is not of the Father, but is of the world. 17 And the world passeth away and the lust thereof; but he that doeth the will of God abideth for ever.*

1 Peter 2: 11 Dearly beloveth, I beseech you as strangers and pilgrims, abstain from fleshly lust, which war against the soul.

Matthew 5: 28 But I say unto you, that whosoever looketh on a woman to lust after her hath committed adultery all ready in his heart.

#8----- Fornication 1 Corinthians 10: 8 Neither let us commit fornication, as some of them committed, and fell in one day three and twenty thousand.

1 Corinthians 6: 18 Flee fornication. Every sin that a man doeth is without the body; but he that committeth fornication sinneth against his own body.

Fornication is sin. It is sin- sexual intercourse between two people who are not married. It is sin -sexual intercourse between two of the same sex. Both can be forgiven of if repented of and turned away from. And marriage will not help them one bit. God will not change his word he created man for woman not man for man.

Ephesians 5: 3 But fornication, and all uncleaness, or covetousness, let it not be once named among you, as becoming saints.

The before mentioned sins are just a few there are more especially in this day and times we live in. Sin will be judged by God, at the judgment, but you can be forgiven before that day. Repent now today, tomorrow is not guaranteed to us, today is the day of repentance. The Lord is merciful and will forgive you, Repent, Turn aside from your sin, Except Jesus Christ as your Saviour, Give yourself totally to him, commit your ways to Him, Study His word, and He will give you eternal life. The secret is to mean it from your heart you can't fool God for He reads your heart.

Ephesians 1: 19 And what is the exceeding greatness of his power to us-ward who believe, according to the working of his mighty power

Chapter 11

GOD'S GRACE IN ACTION

In our lives we have very few things we can rely on as being true facts. We have a saying is there any truth in it? There is very little we can believe in or on. I think there is only one thing I can believe in that is the word of God. At one time If a person told you something you could bank on them to do what they said they would do. It is said a man only has his word and his word was his bond. Now people do just what they have to do to get the paycheck. I find people have changed so much they no longer care to be pleasant when talking to people. They lack respect they do not take pride in doing their work its just a job and they just do it and get out of there.

People are no longer sensitive to others, their families and children. I think it is because people have strayed from the word of God and the love of God they have become lovers of themselves. *2 Timothy 3: 2 For men shall be lovers of their own selves, covetous, boasters, proud, blasphemers, disobedient to parents, unthankful, unholy, with out natural affections, truce breakers, false accusers, incontinent, fierce, despisers of those that are good,. Traitors, heady, high minded, lovers, of pleasure more than lovers of God;*

When I worked I was a professional nurse. I carried my self in a professional manner, acknowledging God in all things. I spoke to people with respect, with compassion, I loved people every thing as done to the best of my ability and to the glory of God. I have had a chance to observe today's nurses. There is a complete difference in their demeanor, I want to give credit where credit is due. The schools of nursing are very technical requires nursing oath also with next century technology I suppose due to the automation of this day and time

This Little Light Of Mine

learning was more difficult have to admit you have to have the knowledge to succeed in this field also the Love of God. This applies to the Doctor also. I feel in these fields you are being used by God more than any other field. It is God's wisdom to you that allows you to do what you do. He has placed you in position to help others. The ministry of Helps is a very important ministry, nursing is a find field to be in.

A Medical Doctor is a highly respected profession that requires the taking of the Hippocratic Oath. People put their lives in their hands and depend on them to use their knowledge to save their lives or to depend upon their years of medical knowledge to prescribe the medicine and treatment they need. I believe there is a great respect given by the majority of those in this great profession to the great physician, Jesus Christ.

In my lifetime I can say most physicians I have had to treat me have been tops in their field and God fearing professionals. Including those I have had the opportunity to work with. I have said all this to get to the real point of this Chapter. We are living in a time when people of all professions and non professions, at the top or at the bottom disregard the life of others. I have just heard on the television that more people die in the hospital from mistakes made by professional staff than people that die of Cancer or High Blood Pressure.

When you are admitted or walk into a hospital you do not know if you will walk out. I am going to tell you of a man who walked into a hospital and I want to let you know God has the last word. The man was 62 years old. Born Downs Syndrome he had never been in a hospital since he was a baby. He was a full term baby, delivered in the hospital the mother was told he would not live long. His diagnosis was he was born with Developmental Problems. He was three pounds at birth he was carried on a pillow his vessels were transparent and could be seen he was very fragile, the hospital staff worked on him to keep him alive day and night. His mother was sent home after the proper time, but the baby remained for weeks in the hospital. The mother was finally told the baby would have to go to another hospital where they can properly take care of his condition, that she would not be able to take care of him. That was a hard decision for the mother and father to make but they did. It was the prayers of the family that the lived. He grew with the love of God and the people that cared for him. He learned to walk after a along time but never was able to talk. He was severely retarded, he was taught to feed himself after years and go to the toilet. He lived in a hospital specially for the care of people like him, a State Institution forty of his 60 years. His family

49

supported him through the years he was there. They would travel the distance to visit him often. He loved his family and his family loved him our hearts were broken to see him like he was. When he grew older the family would get him for family gatherings he was never excluded in any way from the family loved him the more and they let him know it.

He was placed in a home when it was decided by the State to close the Hospital. He loved the home and the people in the home loved him. He was a walking testament of God's love. He showed love to everyone he came in contact with. He was in the group home for about ten years. Every one in the group home went to work. The jobs were jobs that needed to be done at the level the people could do them, mainly putting things in packages. He love going to work. He was willing to join others with joy never displayed anger.

He was a person the Lord healed because he saw a person who he could to show others the love of God. He was not tainted with hate for another, polluted with sin of any kind. Pure in body, soul, and spirit. who learned to praise the Lord by raising his hands to heaven and say Jee use. A angel the Lord has put here for people that have normal intellect to be an example of what God meant by his holiness. He loved the smallest things like very little balls that we kept a supply for him. He knew each ball he had, he knew how many he had, he put then in special order, he had as many balls he wanted in his pocket and in his hands. Those balls were his only treasures on earth.

This special person became ill one day, the home called his brother to notify him. His brother went immediately to the home and the paramedics were going to take him to the hospital, but the brother took him to the hospital they suggested. He walked in and was admitted with the diagnosis of Pneumonia. The doctor came and examined him and said he had pneumonia and would have to stay for treatment. He was assigned a room and transferred from the Emergency area to that room. One of the people that worked at the home came to be with him for love is contagious. The doctor came and examined him and diagnosed him with pneumonia.

He did the usual blood work and what is called a workup, that is everything he needed to evaluate his condition to begin medication an treatment. He ordered bed rest, IV therapy, soft diet, a collection of sputum, no one came to collect it. came in to obtain it and we were there for hours. My brother and I decided to leave for he seem to be sleepy and needed to rest. The dietitian department bought him a tray of food but we told her not to give him that food it was a meal we might eat, but he could not eat that food. We felt we should let him rest and we would come back later. When we left he was smiling, he was happy and trying to talk his way to his friend from the home, She said she would stay with him. We left and went home shortly after we were home my brother got a call from the friend we left at the hospital with him. We dropped everything and met at the hospital, what a shock we found when we got there. He had been taken to the Critical Care Unit, when we got there we were so shocked I was breathless the nurses were busy with him we asked the lady what happened we had just left him. She told us they brought another food tray for him a very soft diet he began to eat and aspirated the food into his lungs he stopped breathing and was put on a respirator to breath for him. When I went into the room I saw him on al the machines necessary to save his life.

The nurses were cold to us with no response not telling us what happened to him. I know they were busy, but we were there all day and no acknowledgement of our presence. This went on for four days. The fourth day we were there early and the doctor came in he told my brother he wanted him to sign for him to have some treatments and a spinal tap, I could not understand why he just decided to do these test and procedures that should been done when he put him on the ventilator. I asked why he did not put a PICK. A PICK was a new word but the procedure was not new to me it was installing a CENTRAL LINE that you can install antibiotics etc. and anything you need in order to save the veins from IV's.

When I ask why he had not put one in earlier I didn't like his response 'you should have told me to put one in' my response was 'you are suppose to be the doctor why didn't you do it?' I know you didn't think he would live three days so you decided it would not be needed, but God Has the Last Word you don't. Never underestimate any one he did not know I was a professional nurse and I knew.

Prayer answer by God is what I contribute to this young man being raised up from the dead alive and doing well and up on his two feet to be a testimony of God's grace and mercies and no matter who say's you need to be taken out or he has no purpose on this earth in his condition who are you to make that decision the word say's. ***Psalms 105: 15 Touch not my anointed and do my prophets no harm.*** Thank you Lord for leaving him here to remind us how you want us to live on this earth to show others your love and that we should be like a little child. For this young man is my brother I named him Paul Anthony Byrd.

Be careful for nothing, but in everything by prayer and supplication
with thanksgiving let your request be made known unto God.
Philippians 4: 6

Chapter 12

GOD HAS THE LAST WORD

When I awoke this morning I was so full of thanksgiving to the Lord God our creator and to the Lord Jesus Christ our Savior for all his goodness and mercies toward me. I am going to quote a saying I am sure you have heard many times before. "You don't know like I know what the Lord has done for me," and "oh what a day a day of thanksgiving to me." He has saved me, he has kept me, he has healed me, and this is what I want to tell you about. It is the a day before Thanksgiving even though I am grateful every day is a day of thanksgiving.

I just want to expound upon this Thanksgiving day that is upon me.
In view of this day I feel I should bear my soul my way of giving thanks to the Lord in this manner. We know we are our heavenly fathers children and we know he watches over us. I am a little more aware he watches over me then maybe most people are for he careth for me.
As you continue to read on you might agree with me or you might disagree. Usually every one has a way of getting together with the ones they love and celebrate this holiday with gestures of love toward that person, or people. Most often by feeding them too much of their favorite food or spending time remembering when.

It would be my most gratifying enjoyment for me to give thanksgiving and praise to my Lord and my Savior for all his goodness and mercies to me all this day, and all the other days he has given me. For its the grace and mercies of the Lord that I am alive to see this Thanksgiving day. This time last Thanksgiving I was in such a great deal of pain in my back. I thought I

This Little Light Of Mine

would have to become dependent upon a wheel chair to be able to get around. It was painful just to put my foot one in front of the other, through the pain I continued thanking the Lord for all that he was doing for me daily just being alive made me so grateful and thank full.

I am putting emphases on Thanksgiving as a special day because it is the one day people think of to give thanks to their Creator. This is well and good but after Thanksgiving day the next few days Thanksgiving to our Creator is put on hold. Now this does not apply to all of us, but to the majority of the human creation. ***Philippians 4: 6 Be careful for nothing; but in every thing by prayer and supplication with thanksgiving let your request be made known unto God.***

People in the church or out of the church find little time to give God thanks.
You do not have to wait until you get into trouble to give God trouble anytime is the right time to give God thanks. If you are not going through something, now you probably just come through something, or getting ready to go through something.
We all can find something to thank God for. I am so conscious of my goodness from the Lord that I find it necessary to give God thanks when I awake in the morning, all during the day and when going to bed at the end of the day. When I think of the goodness of Jesus and all he has done for me, my very soul cries out Halleluiah thank God for saving me.

The Lord has bought me through so much in my life time I have so much to be thankful for. I have had a great deal of grief in my life. I lost a dear brother who was married to a woman that had 3 sons, they had been married for years and her boys were in prison they got out. His wife's sons did not like her being married. An argument came up and one of shot my brother in the head, while she looked on. There was no charges bought against them or her. My first husband died of Cancer of the Lungs. I lost my baby girl as a young woman to Lupus. She had a son and a baby I was already raising the son, but the baby another son was adopted by a friend of hers. Months after she died I lost my second husband from a heart attack. I lost my father at the age of 94 from Cancer of the Lungs. Two years later I lost my Mother at the age of 97 years my father and mother were married 70 years. I lost my first son a young man to Cancer of the liver they were all saved when the Lord took them home.

If it were not for the Lord on my side I would be dead. I was in a very bad accident years ago and was thrown through the wind shield I was in a coma for a few days I lost the use of my right arm and hand. My scalp dropped down over my forehead and my forehead dropped down over my eye. I thought at the time I had lost my eye sight in the left eye. I remember the doctor had a specialist in to test my eye. He said I had not damaged my eye, it looked worst then it was. The Lord healed the whole forehead up so well that after a long while (months and months)you can barley see a slight swollen forehead. I had a fractured bone in my hand, and had surgery on my hand. He healed it completely after surgery.

My arm was a little longer healing. The arm was limp and useless. I could not lift it, I could not wash dishes, bath or anything. I could do nothing the arm and the hand was useless. The hand was closed and I could not open it. It was probably a nerve involvement the doctor suggested I go to Physical Therapy I went for several weeks until it hurt so bad I couldn't stand it. My hand would not open and they would pry my fingers opened. A Pain Specialist explained I would have to have a special treatment to resolve this condition. He would have to put a needle in the front of my neck to reach the back of my neck to hit the nerve that controls the nerve to release my right hand. If I didn't have this procedure my arm will wither. When the doctor said the word withered, I recalled the Lord healed a man with a withered arm in the bible. I told the doctor I was not going to let him put a needle into my throat and reach the back of my neck to heal me, I told him I was not going to have the procedure I was going to trust the man that healed the man with the withered hand in the bible. I believed the Lord to heal me.

Sometime the Lord does things in his way that is not like our way. It took several months, but I continued to trust the Lord, and moved my hand and arm as much as I could with great pain. In his word he said he is not a respecter of people what he did for one he would do for me. Moving my arm and hand slowly and painfully I was able to move it more and more. At this time my son had to care for me and my granddaughter, his daughter for she had a broken arm too, and could not move it. We both was in the same bed and my son took care of us, cooking and everything we needed, for we were helpless from that accident, If it was not for the Lord we would have died.

It was a long time, but God's time is different then our time. He said a day is like a thousand years to him. Finally I was shocked one day when I was able to use my dish rag to wipe over my dishes. I was so thankful I cried and thanked the Lord. I was beginning to see the arm moving more and I was able to do more with my hand. Eventually I could dress myself and do other things. Soon I was able to lift my arm, and move my hand opening it and closing it to where it was normal as before. Thanksgiving is due to the Lord for healing us.

Philippians 4: 6 -7 Be careful for nothing; but in every thing by prayer and supplication with thanksgiving let your request be made known until God. And the peace of God, which passeth all understanding, shall keep your hearts and minds through Christ Jesus.

Psalms 84: 11- 12 No good thing will he withhold from them that walk uprightly Oh Lord of host, blessed is the man that trusted in thee.

Chapter 13

You Can Live Without a Man

I was reluctant about writing this Chapter because people (woman) would not like to hear this. I can just hear the many critics being verbal. Why would she want to write about such a subject? Some say it is a subject too close or too personal to discuss. many may say; I don't believe God wants me to be alone. He says to marry and multiply that's true. Marriage first. woman to man, and man to woman. usually the first thing a woman says is I haven't run into a man yet. Don't try to run into one, let him run into you. I will continue to look until I find a man. There are so many things said about why you are not successful and do not have a man. Women seem to ignore or don't want to face the real meaning why you don't have a man.

I am going to talk to you very frank because the Lord would want me to be honest, and in the Spirit when I discuss this subject. This is not always excepted what I am going to tell you It is not what I say, it is what the Lord says. I am going to speak to the (born again Christian and to the unsaved) Man and Woman, Seek you first the Lord and he will give you the desire of your heart. If you are wise you will take this road if unwise you will do what you want to do. Deception will be your fate.

If you have not allow the Lord in your life to prepare you for a life close to him first you cannot find the man best suited for you. If it is not Gods time or Will for you to have a husband Satan will set you up with one (a man) the wrong one. You won't know it is the wrong one until he begin to show his true self.

Did you know you should be prepared by the Lord to find a man?

56

This Little Light Of Mine

You have to be prepared for a man, especially if it is the man the Lord has for you, a man of God. Women always say they want a man that is in church or they will tell you I will go to church to see if I can find me a man. In the same way men go to church to get a woman. This is because subconsciously you want to get a Christian man because a Christian man would have all good qualities, <u>wrong</u> Some men in the church are of the same quality as the men in the street. This is why I try to impress upon you unless the Lord is in you the man you get might not be the man you want. I will tell you there are some men in the church that will have no respect for you and will mistreat you, just like the men in the street. If you are not rooted and grounded in the Lord you cannot tell the difference. If you live a life controlled by the Lord, finding the right man is like finding a needle in a hay stack. It is a hard thing that's why you have to listen to what the man says to you. If he is married say to him so long go home to your wife. That is going out the world backward, more to loose than gain.

I would like to plead with you to never get involved with a man in prison. I understand a friend you meet will want you to meet a man that is in prison and is very nice and is lonely and needs someone to visit him as a friend. She will entice you to go with her while she visits someone else in the prison, but she will tell you to visit this guy who is a friend. How would feel if you knew someone lonely in prison? You would feel sorry for him. She knows that. The prisoner she introduce you too knows just what to say to you he will pled with you to continue to visit him. Play on your goodness and your compassion for people. Tell him you can not get involved with a man in prison, and you want to have a friend that can keeps you busy outside of prison.

This is a true story I will share with you, of what can happen if you are not aware of his craftiness that he has all day and all night to plan what to tell a good person like you. He is a expert con man.

This happened to this very nice compassionate lonely single young Christian women. The prisoner she was introduced to was a older man then she was, and had been sentenced to twenty five years in prison, he did not tell her what he did, or any thing about himself. She felt he should not be there, so she continued her visits. A older women pleaded and begged her not to visit this man for there were no life with him. Pray for him but, do not go to see him any more. She continued to visit him for years. She was talked into marriage, against what the older woman told her. He had fifteen years to do before his release. She was imprisoned along with him as if she was behind those bars. She supported him while he was there, she waited for him to get out of prison

57

for almost twenty years. In the time, she paid visits where they were allowed to be intimate. She supported him financially. He never told her how much time he was sentenced too or what he did to be in prison.

I am a relative to this young lady and loved her dearly, I am the old women that told her not to marry him. She had been married to this man for fourteen years. She was convinced to marry him and keep the secret. She told me she was going to visit him earlier and I told her to stop going up there. She told me about him, then she told her mother. I wondered why she showed no interest in dating or finding a men out in society. With talking to her I found out this deep secret. She made herself except the position she was in. To me this is a form of abuse(mental)She worked and took care of him and drove many miles to the prison to visit him. I asked her if she loved him and she said she was making the best of her wrong choice. I suggested she divorce him in prison there would less problem getting a divorce if he was still there. I tried to get her to see when he comes home she will have a real problem on her hands in many ways. Well she found out; When he was released she bought him home to her two bedroom apartment she shared with her daughter and her daughter's son age seven years old. She lived in a project apartment on the fourth floor. She told me she had no feeling sexually for him since he is out. He is unable to find a job to help her, she works two jobs her daughter does not work and does not get any support for her son. She has no extra money coming into the home. So she has four people to take care of. He has daily contact with his prison friends in his old neighborhood for they are released from prison also and keep in touch with each other daily. Instead of working they hang out.

In telling you this I hope it will help someone to avoid the same mistake, I pray they will listen. A man that has been incarcerated that long at the age this old man was will find it hard to adjust to outside living, work after these many years and a prison record he will unlikely get a job in most cases. This is a situation you don't want. She talks to women groups now to let them understand the mistakes in this situation. She has to pay a lawyer to obtain a divorce. It could have had a different turn of event for her. She being single could have met a good man to love her, worked for her, bought her a house and moved her into and out of the project. She would have been free, and happy as a husband and wife situation.

I would like to share with you what to consider when looking for a husband:

Make sure he is committed to Jesus. Listen to what his conversation is about. Is he saved and in love with Jesus?

You can not change A man. KEEP THIS FACT FOR MOST IN YOUR MIND. If you feel you have to change him let him go early, save yourself from headache and heartache. You can never change a man, only God can change a man. If he has been incarcerated let him go. If he found Christ in Prison let him prove himself, by continued service to the Lord for a long time, be careful.

Make sure he is committed to the church. Does he help in the church? Is he faithful in his attendance? If he says lets go to the park on the second Sunday after you met, ease away from him.

Does he attend Bible class Wednesday nights? This will tell if he wants to learn the word of God and if he desires to hear the word of God. He will apply the word he will want to live the word.

Make sure he loves his mother. If he does not love his mother and treat her with respect he will not love you or respect you. This is a very important point for you to know. Believe me this is the truth don't ignore this point. Also his sister and the females in the family. Some men have no respect for women.

Does he have a job? Is he working on a job? Is it a good well paying job? If it is a car wash job you know he will not be paid for rainy days, make sure he has been on his job at lease five years or more. Make sure his earnings can support you comfortable. If you work make sure your money does not have to pay the bills. Work to afford extras not necessity. Find out how he spends his money does he pay his bills on time each month? Make sure he pays his Tithes and offerings cheerfully every Sunday.

A main issue to be aware of his age. I hear you say what difference does that make when you are in love. First mistake I made. Age is very important in a marriage or courtship.

My dear from experience I feel the Lord would have me to talk to you about the age issue. If you are of the age eighteen and you met this man of thirty two I would suggest you be very kind to him introduce him to your father and leave him alone. The act of introducing him to your father let's him know (that you and your father have communicate, and your father knows who he is). It is for your protection, if you are of a older age, and meet a male make sure he is able to retire from a very good job. Do not be interested unless he has been on his job over ten years and has a pension plan also for older couples make sure his Social Security monthly income payment is more than two thousand dollars per month. Stay within your own age group. Leave young men to the younger woman.

Older men sometimes are very possessive and can be cruel, and have a tendency of making you his servant, and so many other things that are unpleasant. Why ? because he is more experienced in what to do with a women. He has had experience with women and knows how to get his way about things that may not be to your liking. A man that is old can't get a women his age because they in most cases are aware of his tricks and she won't go along with him in his attempt of superiority, so he goes for younger inexperienced woman.

My suggestion is if you have a man you are interested in I would introduce him to your Pastor and let them talk to gather. What ever your Pastor say about him is probably right.

Now the same things I have pointed out what to look for in the man applies to you too. Can I recommend that you always maintain a quality of respect about yourself as a Christian woman. Let the man be leading even if we know what is coming next. Men always want to feel they are ahead of us. If you are a wise women you will let him believe that. I believe you should look well dressed from the inside out.. I mean your under garments should look and fit you as well as your outer garments. I believe you should wear bras that fit you properly, the same with under garments. You don't represent a Christian woman with your bust hanging out or you navel and behind hanging out under a short blouse. etc. A woman that dresses like a lady does not have to worry about her husband admiring other women. The Bible tells us we must dress modestly. The closer you are to the Lord the better you represent the Lord, and his will not yours. I want to tell you until you are married under no circumstances should the bed be entered into your relationship. Put the bed in the right place!!

I cannot express this enough if you are a Christian woman or man the word tells you under any circumstances should the bed be part of your relationship until marriage. ***Ephesians 5: 3 But fornication, and all uncleanness, or covetousness, let it not be once named among you, as becometh saints: Galatians 5: 16 Walk in the Spirit, and ye shall not fulfil the lust of the flesh. 24 And they that are Christ's have crucified the flesh with the afflictions and lusts.***

Your prayer life says a lot about you as a child of God, and your relationship

This Little Light Of Mine

with the Lord. It also puts you in the position to hear the voice of the Lord in your life. This helps you to operate in the way of the Lord, and you will know how to run your household and children.

Let the Lord save and mold him into the man he wants you to have. I want you to know the Lord knows the heart of the man and he knows your heart. You cannot deceive the Lord.
The truth of the matter depends on where you are in your relationship with the Lord. Your relationship with the Lord determines weather the Lord can trust you to be true to Him or will you allow Satan to overpower you and you succumb to your lust for a man. Love is not lust Love comes from respect one for another first.

What we can do to please one another and make each other happy. These efforts are very important early to a relationship. This is important that these things are well on their way to being accomplished before sex enters the relationship. Sex before marriage puts marriage on hold and speeds up an end of a relationship that needed to be in controlled obedience.
Disobedience to God's Law causes a brake down of relationship and Satan creeps into and destroys God's plan for happiness.
2 Samuel 11: 3 And David sent and enquired after the woman, And one said, is this Bathsheba, the daughter of Eliam, the wife of Uriah the Hittite? And David sent messengers, and took her; and she came in unto him, and he lay with her; for she was purified from her uncleanness: and she returned unto her house. We know the rest of the story there are several stories of lust, and the sequences of pregnancy and failure written in the Bible. True repentance is in order, Hope for forgiveness.

Christ made woman out of man but he did that so woman would know their place in God, and to keep us closer to him so we wouldn't think we were too wise. Woman have a special thing about them that came from the Lord. This makes us a little ahead of the male when we follow the Lord it is a special gift he has given woman. That is where the saying there's a good woman behind every good man. A wise woman knows that, but is smart enough not to let the man know it. I think this is the time to say to you women you are not ready for (the) man the man God wants you to have..

Before the Lord gives you a man he will prepare you for him and him for you. Ladies you have to be in touch with God first then yourself before you can portray your self to someone that probably has one thing in mind.
I would suggest you get as close to God if you are praying to the Lord to give

61

you a man (a husband). That would be the first move and the foremost step to start with. When you get on one accord with the Lord and you cry out as Mary did "My Soul does Magnify the Lord," and mean it, than you may be on the right track. Most woman prepare their body with seduction and sexual wardrobes for a man that you want but, not the one that is for you. The same preparedness to get one is the same way you can prepare to do with out one. It depends upon where you are with Christ in both cases. Obedience is the key in both cases. If you believe God will give you a man and the man he wants you to have when he wants you to have him. You are a wise woman and the Holy Spirit has given you that wisdom.

When you are in Christ you will carry yourself in a manner that is pleasing to the Lord and the right man. If you dress in a exposed manner with your dress up to your buttocks, and your breast uncovered hanging down to your knees this is not pleasing to a man God would give to you. Do you see what I mean? If your mouth speaks curses, or your mouth look as if it was a top of a bottle of opened booze, you would attract that other kind of man you know who's choice (Satan's) and yours.

I am a living Testament of how the Lord can give you the man for you or he can keep you without a man. Yes I did say He can keep you with out a man. He has done it for me and he will do it for you. If you stay in his will for your life or go out of his will and disobey him. I was a young girl preparing to graduate High School. I loved the Lord, I was obedient to my parents, never a problem to them I loved my family and had a happy childhood. One day a man came up to me while I was waiting for the bus to go home from school he was attending the high school under the G, I. Bill of Rights.

He began to talk to me and my life was completely changed. He was eleven years older than me. He had been to the Army and around the world. I disobeyed my parents and God, and married him. The sin of my life, I discussed this marriage in great detail in my first book in fact Chapter 1. After four years of marriage I had the first of our three children, two boys and a girl. Divorced after almost ten years of an abusive marriage.

So don't think you are beyond Satan's attempt to cause you to fall from God. At this point I will share a thought I have that is I believe this might be that the fleshly desire for man- woman is the number one trap Satin uses to cause men and woman to fall into sin. *Galatians 5: 19 Now the works of the flesh are manifest, which are these; Adultery, fornication, uncleanness, lasciviousness,* Remember the way to get your man to marry you keep him out of the bed. The man I married and I had nothing in common, the word tells us not to be unequally yoked, that was what I was. He was an alcoholic when I met him, he had numerous women in his life before me. He was my first date. Satan had me, and turned all my Godly principles around. I disobeyed my God and listened to the voice of Satan.

Make sure you are both yoked with God.

Ten years after the divorce the Lord reclaimed me in the Church. I took my children to New York and I went back to the Lord repented. I enrolled in a Moody accredited Bible Institute for twelve years. I was so happy learning and serving the Lord in New York. After thirty five years without a male relationship the lord sent me back to my hometown to take care of my mother and father. After six years in my home town the Lord blessed me with a husband that the Lord gave to me. There were thirty five years before the Lord gave me my second husband a true man of God. A man that loved me in grade school. I did not know who he was when we met. He revealed this to me later. Do you see how God works, he loved me in grade school set behind me in class and pulled my ribbons on my braids. God knew this and had him for me. He had a heart attack and went to Glory six years later. It has been fourteen years ago. He loved me very much left me too soon.

The Lord has kept me since without the desire for another man I am still in love with my husband. I am a widow indeed *1 Timothy 5: 5 Now she that is a widow indeed, and desolatete, trusteth in God, and continueth in supplications and prayers night and day.* Because of my love for the Lord, I do not seek to be involved with another husband unless the Lord says difference in my future. I am happy and have the peace and joy of the Lord in my life. *Hebrews 12: 21 Make you perfect in every good work to do his will, working in you that which is well pleasing in his sight, through Jesus Christ; to whom be glory for ever and ever. Amen*

Philippians 4: 7 And the peace of God which surpasses all understanding, shall keep your hearts and minds through Christ Jesus.
Don't say that's good for you but it don't work for me, it will work for you too, if you put the Lord first. If you will remember persistence pays off. *Walk in the Spirit and you will not fulfill the lust of the flesh. Romans 8: 4-8 wait on the Lord wait I say on the Lord.* There are so many things you have to learn about how the Lord works. It is important to remember you must be a Christians in all you do in your relationship in order to keep him in line and build up his belief in Christ. This keeps him happy and keeps the Lord happy. In a way you are responsible for making him your husband a

stronger Christian believe it or not, the Holy Spirit will guide you. What I have previously discussed applies so be careful for a relationship can extend to a long marriage or a short lustful relationship. God instituted marriage between a man and a woman, then children, this is basic but in that order is the will of God.

For the woman that is alone from a separation, divorce, death, or maybe you are waiting for the Lord to give you another husband. Whatever situation you find yourself in you can make it with out a husband if you concentrate upon staying in the will of God If it is his will he will give you another husband or man. Please be mindful of Satan's attempt to turn us away from the love of the law of the Lord. I find he has used our weakness for sex to do just that, that is why we must be obedient to God's laws and to his ways and not ours.

Being happy working for the Lord is such a delight if you are not in a relationship, I want to make it clear to be married is the best position a person can be in to share your life with someone else is good. I was ordained by God to marry a man and multiply with children born is that marriage and nothing less. My Mom and Dad were married for70 years. I am not against marriage but for it, is a beautiful institution, if it's in God's will. Just as beautiful it is to be married it is just as beautiful to be alone with Jesus as your husband if you don't have one. He will be to us what ever you want him to be. You can do it live with out a man only if Jesus is the head of your life.

Philippians 4:11 Not that I speak in respect of want: for I have learned, in whatever state I am, therewith to be content.

Colossians 1: 18 And he is the head of the body, the church: who is the beginning: the firstborn from the dead; that in all things he might have the preeminence.

Chapter 14

Why Don't You Go to Church?

A family that prays to gather stays to gather is a familiar statement expressed usually to get someone to go to church or to get someone to become a believer and be on one accord with family or friends. I know several people that do not go to church. Both say they are saved and love the Lord. I am governed by the scripture that says do not judge. I know some people that did not go to church because they were not ready to live a Christian life. These people are the ones that Satan have such a strong hold on them and have that hold so long that they do not want to live any other way and reject any way of Christianity. That is until their time come to meet their maker, that is when they hear depart from me I never knew you.

Some may have tried at one time or another to attend church and dedicate their lives to the Lord, but they allowed Satan to turn their mind back to his way. The Bible says they returned to their own vomit. The Bible also says when your house is swept clean and you go back into the world you will pick up ten more demons. The Bible say's in *Hebrews 10: 26 For if we sin willfully after that we have received the knowledge of the truth, their remaineth no more sacrifice for sins.*

Many people do not attend Church because they know what is required of them to put Christ first in their lives and some people just can't put him first. This is because they can not realize it is the Lord that gave them all that they have even the breath in their bodies. When the Lord calls people to serve Him they cannot let go of the things they have accumulated their homes, money, material thongs that will rotten away with time, they hold on to these things

65

as if they were the most important thing in their lives. I am reminded of the rich young man that loved the Lord and wanted to follow Christ, but when the Lord told him to leave all that he owned and follow Him he couldn't do it. The word say's you came on this with nothing and you can't carry nothing with you. This is Satan's way of keeping these people in bondage, if you don't come to Christ before you die you will spend Eternity in Hell with Satan.

The Church is the place to come for deliverance, healing for our sin sick souls, strength, to hear the word of God, to learn to love, and we are justified by Faith in God. The word tells us how can you hear with out a preacher. You wouldn't go to a night club to hear a preacher expound the word of God. The Church is a place of producing Spiritually alive members not dead ones. A place where God's people come to stay alive, receive cleansing for their souls, and peace that surpasses all understanding, joy unspeakable and full of Glory from the word of God with the Anointing of God.

Mainly it prepares us for Everlasting life with our Lord and Savior Jesus Christ.

When you are not a member of the Church you are walking dead and don't know it. You have no closeness with your Creator. You have no Spiritual connection, you have no prayer life, no direction, you are full of self, and not of the Holy Spirit you are Spiritually dead. You are just like Sampson when he was in Christ he was full of life and strength, outside of Christ he had no power or strength and death soon followed.

The people who attend Church are living proof of God's word; Blessed are they that hunger and thirst after Righteousness they shall be filled. Going to Church is for living people for they hunger and thirst, dead people don't hunger nor do they thirst, only the alive, their food is found in the Church through the preached word. A Church that is alive is a Church that people attend and are Saved through the Blood of Jesus. A alter call is given and people are drawn by the Spirit of God to Repent, turn from their wicked way, being borne again that is when your spirit is changed, Christ sets up his abode in your temple for you are the temple of the Living God not I but Christ that liveth in me. Speaking in tongues, praying in tongues as the spirit gives utterance communicating with God because He is Spirit. Rejoicing not in how good you are but that your name is written in the Lambs Book of Life. It's all about Jesus and not you.

There are some people who find fault with the Church as a reason why they

This Little Light Of Mine

don't go to Church. They will tell you there are more hypocrites in Church that's why I don't go, if you went you would be one more hypocrite. Another excuse is the people in the church are just like the people I know outside the church. The world is in the church. I know that there are people who are members of Church that are self centered, proud, and boasters of themselves, and not of Christ. People who look to God for blessings of material matter instead of Salvation and Repentance in Jesus name. I hope you know Satan attends Church every time the door opens. Some go to church as if it was was a social club, to make people think they are sincere, but the truth is not there the book say's the Lord is not mocked for what so ever a man soweth that shall he also reap. The Lord will reveal the truth. he will expose you and your motive for the Lord reads the heart. He is Omnipotent, Omnipresent, and Omnisious. He is all power, He is everywhere, He is all knowing.

Hebrews 10: 25 Not forsaking the assembling of yourselves together, as the manner of some is, but exhorting one another, and so much the more, as ye see the day approaching.

Do you know their are things you must be aware of: *You go to church to listen: Attentively to what the preacher is saying, your full attention should be on what is being preached, using your Bible to follow the preacher.
*You go to church to hear the word Expectively: This means you are expecting the Lord to speak to you through the message and give you a word for only you. *You go to church an be Prayerfully: Pray inwardly to the Lord letting him know you are totally submitted to him and his will. Also that you want to live in his will. *You go to church an be Patiently: taken in the value of the preached word not rushing to get out of the service but letting each word be of some value to the life you are committed to live.
* You go to church Humbly: You must have a humble heart for the word of God. You cannot think that you know everything and there nothing you don't know. You will get nothing out of the service. Listen to the word with humbleness.
*You go to church Great fully. You should have an attitude of gratitude for the word preached, gratitude to the Lord for his sacrificial death for your sins. and Salvation.
* You go to church with Purpose: You should have purpose when you are in church. Your purpose is to pray fully ask the Lord to draw you close to him and help you live in truth through his word.
In the day and age we live in it is so evident the world is setting up for the return of the Lord to the earth, he is taking his people up in the rapture of the church. He is taking his people who are members of The Church not a church

every day from every corner of the earth. Knowing this I find myself getting ready for the Lord for when he comes I want to be found in his perfect will. I want to be free of hate of anyone, I want to have love for all people, I ask the Lord to forgive me of all my sins, and if I have done any wrong to any one to forgive me I also want to do what the Lord would have me do to the best of my ability with love, most of all to help others not turn away from God but to turn to God. Man doesn't want to hear about the cross of Calvary, but it was on the cross the blood of Jesus was shed and it is by that blood we are redeemed unto heaven.

These things are what the church is made of and people of God that do these things are what the church is about. The Lord gave us an example of what the church should be like in **Revelation 3: And unto the angel of the church of Sardis write:** Also the church of Philadelphia, and Laodiceans, The Lord corrected, reproved, and laid out the message to the churches. **He that hath a ear let him hear what the Spirit saith unto the churches.**
1 Timothy 3:14 These things write I unto thee, hoping to come unto thee shortly. But if I terry long, that thou mayest know how thou oughtest to behave in the house of God, which is the church of the living God, the pillar and ground of the truth.

Malachi 3: 10 Bring ye all the tithes into the storehouse, that there may be meat in mine house, and prove me now herewith saith the Lord of host, if I will not open you the windows of heaven, and pour you out a blessing, that there shall not be room enough to receive it.

Chapter 15

How do You Feel About Tithing?

Some people make the statement that's all that church wants is your money or they beg to much or that's all they talk about is money or they want me to give them 10% of my pay check they must be crazy or they want to buy the Pastor another new car or people give the Pastor too much he's rich. These are just a few things said about giving tithes. Instead of saying giving tithes I am going to say paying tithes. This is Satan's way of keeping you from being obedient to the word of God. From the beginning of the world people have given tithes on every thing they had no matter how much or how little they had.

This is the most debatable subject in most churches. Each church has a way of dealing with this subject. I am in a simple way going to attempt to teach you what the word of GOD says about tithing that's if you desire to please GOD.

Let us begin with a simple point; The question is are you sincere about serving the Lord according to his will or do you want to serve him according to your will? With that settled we will continue to explain what tithing is. This is for Christians or non Christians straddled the fence and you are bait to be used by Satan. It is up to you to decide weather you want to by Faith choose to believe the word of God. You might have heard some people say I am not going to give in the church because the Pastor has much more then I have, and I am not going to give him any more he should be giving to the people in his church. I would not have you to be ignorant my friend, but do you know the Lord did not make you judge over his ministers, he 's the judge. Most churches have people to take care of the finances taken in and the finances hat is paid out.

In many churches the Pastor is salaried. That means he is paid weekly or monthly whatever, now he has the right to spend his salary the way he sees fit. Just as you spend your salary the way you wish to. Usually the church financial board pays all the bills to keep the church going, and the Pastor does not know how much the bills amount to. The board takes that load off the Pastor so he can be about preaching the word of God. The Tithes or money you give might go anywhere but to the Pastor. The financial board must see to it all money is directed where it is suppose to go and keep accurate records of where each dime went.

The head of the church is the Pastor or Bishop the Lord has in that position if the man is satisfactory for the Lord than he should be satisfactory to the parishioners. It is a good thing to leave the Lord's business to the Lord. I think he has done a excellent job so far.

So many people think of Tithing paying God, that is far from the truth. Don't you know you cannot pay God. You do not have enough money to pay God. He owns every thing The word says he made everything that was made. How can you pay him? Let me tell you if the Lord decide you could not work for a month, what would you do? That's right you would be without work for a month. I would like to tell you I do not tempt the Lord. I cheerfully give my tithes because the Lord is so good to me. The Lord resurrected me out of a bed of death and pain. I could only get up to the bathroom the pain I had was terrible I had to try bedside. For six months I went through this, I could do nothing but say Jesus, I began to sleep at night. the Lord raised me to stand on the side of the bed for one step, no more the pain was too severe in my back. After a year I was able to go to the bathroom with less pain ,but pain. After two years I am able to walk a little further always with pain. If it were not for the Lord healing me, how much would I pay for the healing? You would not be able to afford to pay God ever.

The purpose of Tithing; is being obedient to God's word and acknowledging God as the source of all our earthly goods. Tithing is your Faith in action. The Lord ask for a small amount of 10% of all he gives you on your pay check. or income, how ever you earn your living. He is the one that gives you the strength to make that pay check, or bring in the crop of corn you sold. ***Genesis 28: 22 And this stone, which I have set for a pillar, shall be God's***

house; and of all that thou shalt give me I will surely give the tenth unto thee.

Could you look at giving your 10% to God realizing what he has done for you. When you pay or give your Tithes you are giving to the Lord in obedience to his word, and being obedient to the Lord is about the only thing you can do for the Lord. Beside praising the Lord being obedient is pleasing to the Lord. Obedience to his word that orders us to proclaim the Gospel to all the world in order for the whole world to hear and have the opportunity to come to Jesus and receive Eternal Life. His word says how can you hear without a preacher? The word says the Earth is the Lord's and the fullness thereof the world and they that dwell there in. Why would you have any hesitation when you think of the goodness of the Lord. You give to the Lord. Don't you know he knows when you give and the way you give and how cheerful you give. What happens to your tithe and offering after you give is God's problem not yours. How can you pay 10% of your assets for your health, sight, strength, mind, use of all your limbs, air you breath, waking up every morning and see his sunshine. Think about it; ***Malachi 3:8-10***

Will a man rob God? Yet ye rob me. But ye say wherewith have I robbed thee? In tithes and offerings. Bring all the tithes into the storehouse, that there may be meat in my house, and prove me now herewith saith the Lord of host, if I will not open you the windows of heaven and pour you out a blessing that there shall not be room enough to receive it.

1 Timothy 5: 1 Rebuke not the elder, but in treat him as a father, and the younger men as brothers. The elder women as mothers; the younger as sisters, with all purity.

Chapter 16

GOD IS NOT THROUGH WITH ME YET

When you became a Christian did you believe your life was beginning to be full of happiness, peaceful, and the end of all your problems?

Wrong it is just the beginning. You have turned from a life of sin and Satan has had you doing what he has directed you to do all your life.

Probably things that made you feel good, this is one of the ways he had control over you. All the time knowing you were on your way to Hell.

When you heard the word or the voice of the Lord speaking to your heart and heard your Savior's call you decided you had to make a change in your life and you made the right change from death to life.

A change that will give you everlasting life. In this Christian life you will have tribulation, trials, sickness, sorrow, and temptations of this world, but you will have the Lord on your side. *John 16: 33. These things I have spoken unto you that in me ye might have peace. In the world ye shall have tribulation: but be of good cheer: I have overcome the world.* How encouraging this scripture is to us to know that we have our great God on our side, and he is able to do all things and will bring us through.

What ever your circumstances are in your Christian walk your Faith in God will increase and He will make a way of escape *1 Corinthians 10: 13 There hath no temptation taken you, but such as is common to man; but God is faithful who will not suffer you to be tempted above that ye are able; but will with the temptation find a way to escape, that ye may be able to bear it.*

Remember with all your trials and testing you go through the Lord teaches us

This Little Light Of Mine

what we need is to grow closer to him, let us remember God is not through with us yet.

I want to tell you His love never fails. The Lord is everything you need, in any situation you find yourself in you will find him in the mist of it all and he is right on time. Now He is not only with you when you first decide to follow Him or when you get in the height of your living for the Lord he will be with you in your older years. I some times feel the Lord has forgot my desire to be of a greater service to him in anyway he leads me. He does not do things like we think he should, he might want you to give a blessing of a piece of money to someone, or visit someone that needs encouragement, to pray for someone, or visit the sick. When we are willing, and sincere He will give us what He want us to do. It is my pleasure to work for the Lord ***Titus 2: 2 -3 That the aged men be sober, grave, temperate, sound, in faith, in charity, in patience. The aged women likewise, that they be in behaviour as becometh holiness, not false accusers, not given to much wine, teachers of good things;*** Don't discount the little things that can have a great impact on your grand children always letting them know what the Lord expects of them. I try to tell my grandson Eric he is going to miss me when I go to heaven. At this time he does not think it is a big deal, he forgets I am the one who raised him. Yes you have to live a life with Jesus for your grand children to see..To enforce the fact you can continue living for he Lord even in your old age. Even with your son he feels he has no reason to call you on the phone or send a mothers day card or a Christmas card. The Lord watches you to see how you handle these situation's. He knows you did nothing to cause this situation but you still love him. He is the only child you have living the other two have gone to heaven. He does not know how I pray for him to find the place again with the Lord that he once knew. He was a child minister that the Lord used to save many people in his ministry. My prayer is Lord do not let him be lost. What joy it would be to hear that he has been forgiven, and has been reclaimed by the Lord. I pray the Lord lets me hear that good news before he calls me home. Since this printing I see the Lord work in his life. He continues to play the organ for three churches each Sunday. He has his own prosperous business. Thank you Lord.

Their might be a blessing in monetary value and the Lord wants you to give your church a sizeable amount. Giving gifts to someone for other work in the cause of Christ that has been established. Keep in mind It's only what you do for Christ that is going to count in the end. There are so many things that we can do for the Lord while we are here on this earth. I thankfully will say that the Lord has brought me through the pneumonia I had and was in bed eight weeks. He has brought me through terrible back pain from a bulge in my back also pain from two pinched nerves in my buttocks steaming from my back. I guess I haven't been in good health I can not do the things I would like to do. I love being his hands, eyes, and feet. I desire to be able to do the things he wants me to do. He is not through with me yet nor is he through with you yet. He said in his word he would make us active even in our old age. He is anointing me to write this book for his glory and honor. If you think you don't have to do anything you will find out. The Lord wants you to get close to him, let's begin with prayer, with giving him praise, and just living a life that is pleasing to Him. He will use you in any way, anytime, and where he want too. The Lord can make you active in any area in the church, he is a all knowing God, he knows what he is doing. Age has no limits with God in the word, most people were used by the Lord in their old age. Age to God is just a number He knows what he has for you to do and to accomplish before he calls you home to live with him. All my life I have always wanted this little light of mind to shine every where I go. This is the name he has given me to name this book; This Little Light of Mine so I can let it shine and It can go everywhere I can't go, and reach people I can not reach, giving them the word to lead them to Eternal Life.

1 Corinthians 1: 18 For the preaching of the cross is to them that perish foolishness: but unto us which are saved it is the power of God.

Chapter 17

The Cross Makes the Difference

If it were not for the cross I would be lost. I thank God for the cross, I thank God for Jesus who endured the cross for my sins. Only the blood washed people of God can say this. At the cross, at the cross, where I first saw the light and the burdens of my heart rolled away it was there by faith I received my sight and now I am happy all the day.

People seem to forget the cross it is seldom mentioned anymore I cannot except the thought of not talking about the cross. The cross is the most important fact in our lives, if it was not for the Cross where Jesus died and the Resurrection of Jesus Christ our lives would have no meaning or hope for a life hereafter, we would all have our destination in Hell. We would be drifting like a ship in the sea without a life boat.

Our Lord created the world and all that is in it. We were created in His image and likeness of Christ. Jesus was with the father from the beginning. After creation we fell in sin and was on our way to hell, for sin is the opposite of God who is purity. who loves his creation. Looking at this situation God saw where He needed a Saviour for a sinful world. As he ask Abraham to sacrifice his only beloved son, He appointed his only beloved Son who he loved to die for our sins, a supreme sacrifice of a pure holy son of God for the sins of the world.

Luke 9:23 And he said to them all, if any man will come after me, let him deny himself, and take up his cross daily, and follow me. Our Christian life requires us to take up our cross and live according to the word of God and remember the sacrifice of the Cross. As Jesus approached the Cross we must know he died to save us from our sins. and his resurrection that we might have Eternal life in heaven with our creator.

Philippians 2:7-11 and took, upon him the form of a servant, and was made in the likeness of men. And being found in fashion as a man, he humbled himself, and became obedient unto death, even the death of the cross. Wherefore God also highly exalted him, and given him a name which is above every name: That at the name of Jesus every knee shall bow of things in heaven, and things under the earth;

In a simple manner I will try to give you some idea of what Jesus went through to save our souls from hell. These events are ***called the Passion of Jesus.*** After the Lord had the Last Supper with his Disciples Judas one of them betrayed him. Jesus was then arrested and accused of Blasphemy by the Pharisees, chief priest, and elders, they were the Politicians of that day, and they killed Jesus. The same is the situation today. He was condemned to death the death of the Cross. The Cross-was the cruelest method of dying. It is a slow way of suffocation. They platted a crown of thrones and put it upon his head, a which added to his pain. They spat upon him, mocked him, took his clothes off and as the scriptures was fulfilled when they parted his garments casting lots; They parted my garments among them, and upon my vesture did they cast lots. When they got to Golgotha they gave him vinegar and gall to drink. Then crucified him. They placed a sign upon his head that said This is Jesus King of the Jews. On the Cross the Lord asked his father to forgive them for they know not what they do.` *Hebrews 12: 2 Looking unto Jesus the author and finisher of our faith; who for the joy that was set before him endureth the Cross, despising the shame, and is sat down at the right hand of the throne of God.*

Some people wear the cross around their neck to show empathy for the suffering. The cross is the cruelest way of death. We are not asked by the Lord God to die on a cross only to except the cross as being essential to our Christian Faith. The means of our Eternal Life for if it were not for the Cross we would be hell bound. Because of the Cross we have forgiveness of sin. We have Salvation, Healing, Life Eternal and everything we need in the name of Jesus and by his Blood shed on that cross. Thank You Jesus for your supreme sacrifice for us. Thank you for saving one of the thieves hanging on the cross with you. You instituted the gift of salvation for me if I ask for forgiveness for all my sins that my soul will not be lost. The entire dying upon the cross has a significant meaning for us: We must at one time in our life time experience everything the Lord went through to his death. From precaution, hard tasks,

This Little Light Of Mine

or suffering, Pain, loneliness, isolation, to rejection, all this we must give to God in total submission from our very heart and soul. On the Cross the Lord spoke words which were recorded as his seven last words:

The first word: was his forgiveness of others who had accused him falsely. For he was with out sin but was made sin for us. ***Luke 23: 34 Father forgive them, for they know not what they do.*** This was done for us to know we must forgive those that misuse us or accuse us falsely, or mistreat us in any way form or fashion. It is up to us to forgive others as he forgave us.

The second word: was the request of Salvation to those who repent and ask for forgiveness that their sins are forgiven. The thief that was nailed on the cross on one side of Jesus repented of his sins and acknowledged who Jesus was and asked the Lord to remember him when he came into his kingdom. ***Luke 23: 43*** Jesus said unto him; ***Verily I say unto thee, "today shalt thou be with me in paradise.*** Through Salvation we are saved and are given Eternal life through Jesus Christ.

The third word: ***John 19: 26 Women Behold thy son!*** These words were so important because it showed the Humility of Jesus and also honor to his mother. It is written Honor thy mother and father that your days may be long upon the earth. It seems to be forgotten these days children do not respect their parents as they should for it is written. These words were spoken in respect to his mother. The Lord was looking out that she had someone to look after her and be her son. I do believe this disciple was John for he was right there with Jesus. Jesus loved John and he loved his also loved his mother. He was showing respect for his mother for she was chosen by God to be chosen to be his mother, as we are to respect our mother. The unity of the Church was being put into existence for the new establishment of the Church was to be Spiritual rather then natural. ***Matthew 12: 50.***

John 19: Behold thy Mother. Again we see the humility of Jesus when he gave his mother over to his best friend John. He knew she would be in the best of care she could have. He let it be know he was mindful of his mother to give her the best. The best of care on this earth by a human being John.

The Fourth word: ***Mark 15: 34 Eloi, Eloi lama sa bach tha i?*** MY GOD, MY GOD WHY HAST THOU FORSAKEN ME?

After discharging his last duty on earth by seeing that his mother was taken care of, he turned his attention to his heavenly father. Jesus was at the ninth hour and was tired of this suffering and pain he was experiencing. He knew he was the Son of God and he was fulfilling the word of God but he looked for God to be at his side. The Son of God did not at the time realize he was the bearer of all of our sins and all the sins of the whole world. God is righteous and without sin and there is a separation from righteousness and sin. That is why Jesus thought God had forsaken him actually God did because of this sin separation. The word says you have to come through Jesus to get to God.

The Fifth word: **John 19: 28 I thirst** Jesus wanted us to realize how human he was. The vinegar and gall he was given revived Jesus strength enabling him to cry out I Thirst. The physical need of his suffering escaped his life. He stated a fact rather than voicing an appeal. These words were to make it clear he suffered as human flesh so there would be no question of his humanity.
He thirst in like manner as we do, our bodies need water to sustain us. To a human body water is most essential. His suffering proved his human side as well as his Godliness.

The Six word: **John 19: 30 It is finished** These words were to remember his purpose was to fulfill the word of God and according to the scriptures. He had accomplished all that was to be done on the cross. The atonement for sins, the freedom of Salvation, all that is needed for all humans to endure the living and the death. He had completed what he was nailed to the cross for. Like father I am through suffering for all you have given me to suffer for I have succeeded to do your will.

The Seventh Word: **Luke 23: 46 FATHER, INTO THY HANDS I COMMAND MY SPIRIT.**

When the Lord said these words he was sure he had accomplished the will of his father and he felt he had pleased his father and having said these words, he gave up the Ghost. It was over, all his suffering was not in vain for we have the power to all the Lord died for. There is no reason why we should miss heaven for Jesus paid it all, all to Him I owe, Sin had left a crimson stain, He washed it white as snow. THANK YOU JESUS.

Matthew 24: 35 Haven and earth shall pass away, but my word shall not pass away Psalms 119: 57 Thou art my portion, O Lord I have said that I would keep thy word. Psalm 119: 89 For ever, O Lord , thy word is settled in heaven.

Chapter 18

THY WORD IS EVERLASTING

Maybe you are among the one's that say there is no truth in the Bible, and that it was written by men. Well I hope to help you to know the word is truth and you are right it was written by men that is holy men of God. Whom were directed by God to let you know what the Lord would have do to receive Eternal Life. I have always thought of the words of the Bible as being our road map as we travel through this journey of life. The Lord gave us his word because he loved us and he does no want any of us to be lost to satin and his followers. *Psalm 119: 81 My soul fainteth for thy salvation: but I hope in thy word.*

The word of God is knowledge to our souls, it is help to us when we are in trouble, it is strength when we feel weak, heart broken, or ill. It is our help in whatever situation we find ourselves in. For me the word of God is my everything. I believe the word of God in its integrity and entirety, I believe every word even if it refers to one thing in one scripture and to the same thing in another scripture, I believe it all. *1 Peter 1: 25 But the word of the Lord endureth for ever. And this is the word which by the gospel is preached unto you. Revelation 22: 19 And if any man shall take away from these words of the book of this prophecy, God shall take away his part out of the book of life, and out of the holy city, and from the things which are written in this book. 1 John 2: But whoso keepeth his word, in him verily is the love of God perfected; hereby know we that we are in him.*

John 8: 31-32 Then Jesus said to the Jews that believed on him, If ye continue in my word, then are ye my disciples indeed; and the truth shall make you free.

Chapter 19

Know The Truth

Acting upon an invitation to visit a church in my area I found the church to be small with about 12 people in attendance. As I entered I was greeted by an elderly member who began to tell me how the Lord has been so good to her in her lifetime, the lady was filled with the Holy Spirit. Now some people would have believed the lady to be an old senile worshiper. I felt the Holy Spirit all over her and I tried the Spirit by the Spirit. I was aware the other people there were very quite even when the preacher was preaching. I think I heard one other person or two that made any response to the message that was preached. I felt love in the church.

In the message the preacher continually mentioned to be saved you must be baptized in the name of Jesus and belong to the Apostolic church. With this observation I wish to say I love all people that are in the church and people who are yet sinners. There are so many people who believe that they are not saved because they were not baptized in Jesus name. This non-truth has caused many of people who have just excepted the Lord as their Savior to doubt weather they are Saved. This is a trick of Satan to take the truth mix it with untruth to confuse the people of God, causing confusion in the Church. In doing so the confusion extends to saved Christians causing them to doubt they are saved and have repented of their sins, and excepted Jesus Christ as their Savior after doing this from your heart and soul You are Saved.

The Truth: *Mark 16: 16 He that believeth and is baptized shall be saved, but he that believeth not shall be damned.*
Acts 16: 30 -31 And brought them out, and said, Sirs, what must I do to

be saved? And they said, Believe on the Lord Jesus Christ and thou shalt be saved, and thy house.

Ephesians 2: 8-9 For by grace are we saved through faith; and that not of ourselves; it is the grace of God; not of works, lest any man should boast.

1Corinthians 15: 2-3 By which also ye are saved, if ye keep in memory what I preached unto you, unless ye have believed in vain. For I deliver into you first of all that which I also received, how that Christ died for our sins according to the scriptures.

These truths are brought to your attention to let you know your Salvation does not depend on weather you were baptized in Jesus name only, but if you were baptized in the name of the Father, Son,
and the Holy Ghost. Your salvation is also based upon whether you except the Lord Jesus Christ and repent of your sins you shall be saved. Now I am not saying you are not saved if you have been baptized in all three and in Jesus name for when you were baptized Father, Son, Holy Ghost you were baptized in the name of all three (the Holy Trinity) God the Father, Jesus Christ the Son of God, the Holy Ghost, you are still baptized in Jesus name. If you ask your pastor he will say the name of Jesus if it will make you feel better. I want to tell you if you were baptized in the name of George Washington if you have not truly repented of your sins and truly mean to serve the Lord it does not matter whose name you were baptized in. You are a liar and the word says God hates a liar, and if you went down into the water a dry sinner, you came up a wet sinner.

I believe the scriptures that refer to baptize in the name of Jesus, but I do not find scripture to prove you are not saved if you are not baptized in Jesus name. This was such an issue for some new converts in my church that some people came to the pastor and said we want to be sure we are saved we want to be baptized in Jesus name. His reply was whose name do you believe you were baptized in, they replied Father, Son, Holy Ghost, he said who is the Father, they replied God, he asked who is the Son, they replied the Lord Jesus Christ the Son of the Living God, he said who!! they repeated what they had said he asked them were you baptized in Jesus name? They said yes.

In some churches it is like a power they impose upon people to belong to there church to believe this, but I wonder what the Lord thinks of part of his church forcing this upon his souls that have come into salvation. In the book of Revelation it says; ***Revelation 22: 19 And if any man shall take away the words of the book of the prophecy, God shall take away his part out of the book of life. and out of the holy city, and from the things which are written in this book.***

The truth: ***Matthew 28: 19-20 Go ye therefore, and teach all nations, baptizing them in the name of the Father,***
and the Son, and of the Holy Ghost; Teaching them to observe all things whatsoever I have commanded you; and lo, I am with you always, even unto the end of the world. Amen

John 14: 25-26 These things have I spoken unto you, being yet present with you. But the Comforter, which is the Holy Ghost, whom the Father will send in my name, he shall teach you, all things and bring all things to your remembrance, whatsoever I have said unto you.

There is something else that causes people to be confused in the church that is Gossip about the Bishop, pastor, deacons, sisters, and members, they are guilty of doing everything you can think of, and some things you can't. My question is did you see them? If you did not see them shut up. If you see them go to them with your pastor, tell them what you saw ask them to repent and be Godly sorry and not do it again. You must pray for them and let the Holy spirit deal with them. Do not tell anyone else. Remember judge not. Let the Lord judge them.

Truth***: Exodus 20: 16 Thou shalt not bear false witness against thy neighbour.***
Jude 1: 23-24 And others save with fear, pulling then out of the fire, hating even the garment spotted by the flesh. Now unto him that is able to keep you from falling and present you faultless before the presence of his glory with exceeding joy.

I have found if I don't see any one doing or saying anything that is not becoming a saint I will pray for them that the Lord who reads the heart will make them holy so they can live eternally with the Lord. If I see them I will let them know their conduct is not pleasing to the Lord and to repent and seek forgiveness. Remember the Lord has the last word to say about everyone. If the Lord said it in his word I belief it. Remember the word says you must strive to holiness, to live in heaven. Another thing that is common to dispute is the clothing that is worn in church. No make up don't go to the beauty shop.

The Truth: *1 Samuel 16: 7 But the Lord said unto Samuel, look not on his countenance, or on the height of his statue; brcause I have released him: for the Lord seeth not as man seeth; for man looketh on the outward appearance, but the Lord Lord looketh on the heart.*

John 7: 24 Judge not according to the appearance, but judge righteous judgment.

1 John 3: 2 Beloveth now we are the sons of God, and it doth not yet appear what we shall be; but we know that when he shall appear , we shall be like him: for we shall see him as he is.

There are some people that say there is no place call hell. They even referred to living in hell now in this day and time.

The Truth: *Matthew 5: 22-29 10: 28 The Greek Gehenna THE place of punishment. (HADES) Matthew 10: 28 and fear not them which kill the body, but are not able to kill the soul but rather fear him which is able to destroy both soul and body in hell.*
Hades -Lartarus: The abode of the dead. Matthew 16:18 And I say unto thee, That thou art Peter, and upon this rock I shall build my church: and the gates of hell shall not prevail against it.

Hebrew word for Hell is Sheol The grave or unseen state. *Psalm9: 17 The heathern shall sink down in hell, and all the nations that forget God. Psalm 116: 3 The sorrows of death compassed about me, and the pains of hell gat hold upon me; I found trouble and sorrow.*

Mark 9: 43 And if thy hand affend thee, cut it off , it is better for thee to enter onto life mained, than having two hands to go into hell, into the fire that never shall be quenche

2 Peter 2: 4 For if God speared not the angels that sinned; but cast then down ro hell, and delivered thewn into chains of darkness, to be reserved unto judgment;

There is another doubt that people have that is questioned; and that is weather there is a devil or satin?

The truth:

83

THE TRUTH: *Hebrew 2: 14 Forasmuch then as the children are partakers of flesh and blood, he also himself likewise took part of the same. that through death he might destroy him that had the power of death, that is the devil;*

1 John 3: 8 He that commitheth sin is of the devil; for the devil sinneth from the beginning. For this purpose the Son of God was manifest that he might destroy the works of the devil.

Ephesians 6: 5 For we wrestle not against flesh and blood, but against principalities, against powers, against the rulers of the darkness of this world, against spiritual wickedness in high places.

People have said there is no Holy Ghost:

The Truth: *Matthew 12: 31-32 And whosever speaketh a word against the Son of man " It shall be forgiven him: but whosoever speaketh against the Holy Ghost it shall not be forgiven him, neither in this world, neither the world to come.*
Wherefore I say unto you, All manner of sin and blasphemy shall be forgiven unto men; but the blasphemy against the Holy Ghost shall not be forgiven unto man.
Revelation 3: 2o Behold I stand at the door , and knock; if any man hear my voice and open the door, I will come in to him, and will sup with him, and he with me.

Chapter 20

GET READY, GET READY, GET READY

YOU MUST BE BORN AGAIN THAT IS IF YOU WANT TO LIVE IN HEAVEN. That is the decision you have to make. If you have not made that decision do not delay make it today. We are living in the last days and the Lord could come and take his church out at any time. Don't you see the signs pointing to his coming? *James 4:7 Submit your self to God. Resist the devil and he will flee. Drew nigh to God and he will draw nigh to you. Cleanse your hands ye sinners, and purify your hearts, ye double minded.* **Don't just read these words you know you need to give your heart to the Lord right now.** Do it right now. Ask the Lord Jesus Christ to forgive you of all your sins and <u>mean it and he will hear you. Now you must mean it and be truthful to God for he reads your heart and he knows when you are telling the truth.</u>

You cannot lie the Lord he knows everything about you he created you. Get ready Get ready Get ready is the call for you to make sure you will be ready when the Lord comes. Don't think you will escape his coming you cannot run far enough he will find you when he comes. His coming will find the rich, the poor, the great, and the small. Don't count on the mountains to protect you they will be moved into the sea. You must be ready when he comes. This is my plea to you Get ready Get ready Get ready to meet the Lord when he comes. Do you know when the Lord comes for you, if you are not ready you will be sent to burn in the Lake of fire. You will not be able to go to heaven because none but the pure in heart, and those who are holy can enter into heaven, There is no impurity in heaven. There is no second place so the only place is either heaven or hell. Lake of fire was made for the devil and his false prophets, the Lord died on the cross, he made it possible for us not to go there, but to live in heaven and have ever lasting life.

At this point I would like to interject this important fact God is love and to get to heaven you must have love. Love for your neighbor, family, and people you come in contact with in your lifetime. It is hard to love people that do you harm, but you have to forgive them and love them. The Lord has impressed upon me that heaven is love and love is the key to heaven. I you have heart in our heart we must ask forgiveness, and replace hate with love for God is love. He tell us if you don't love the people (your brother) who you see, how can you love God who you have not seen.

Chapter 21

A Silhouette of a Angel

A human profile of a Angel.

Weather we accept it are not
Weather we understand it or not
Weather we know it are not
God uses Angles to help us

In my feeble attempt or effort I will do my best to describe a true angel to you. In my following words I hope you will also be able to see this is a true description of a human angel. You are probably saying how does anyone know how to describe a human Angel, well I am going to describe to you when one was born, what one looks like, and how one act to begin with.

It was a beautiful sunny day in June when two prime babies were born to a young girl and a young man in Booth Memorial Hospital in Queens, New York. There were actually two twins born, one a boy, and a girl. The babies were primes, seven months, two pounds apiece. The boy died and returned to God. The little girl lived, but began a life dependence upon miracle, after miracle from God. To describe this tinny baby I will begin by saying she was a handful of baby. She was placed upon a pillow and placed into an incubator, where little crying was heard. Her veins were visible and able to be traced through the body. The skin was thin, transparent, and in a not ready to be born appearance. She was fed intravenously the duration of her stay in the intensive care unit in Pediatrics. Her stay was months with prognosis might live and might not. This decision was clearly in the hands of the Lord. All was being done to let her live. The fact of her being alive was a miracle in it's self, that she was not taken with her brother. Her life continued to be a miracle for months and months. The day she first took a teaspoon of Pre-Soy be milk was a celebration in the pediatric unit. The nurses actually celebrated by drinking milk, We were so happy she was almost a year old. She was able to go home. That caused a great stress for me, for I knew her mom would have a big task taking proper care of her. I was working full time and would be of little help to her. At this time I wanted to give her back to the Lord in thanksgiving for this miracle We had such a beautiful baby blessing service at Bethel Gospel Tabernacle in Jamaica, N. Y. At this service I thanked the Lord for her and the miracle he gave us. To me she was such a special child so close to me, a special bonding for me to her. I know it was God moving in her little life, that is what made me so great full to God Almighty. I looked at her healing that was a miracle in it's self, for her slow-ness was being healed from above.

Being led by the Lord I was very instrumental in getting the proper care for her. She required special care for she was very slow in every phase of life. Being in the Nursing Profession I was alert to most of the options she had for special care and persuaded them to her availability. The doors were opened for her to progress.

There was not a doubt in anyone's mind she was a special baby she was slow in eating, taking her bottle was a test of patience, also the adjustment of living out of the hospital, and slowly growing at her pace. She was late crawling, and much later walking. She had a hard time adjusting to learning everything. She cried about everything and was afraid to try new things. I poured more love out to her and taught her so much with love. It seemed to me I could not do enough for her and at this time I took her full time to raise her. I enrolled her in a school for children her age while I was at work and it worked out fine. At this time her mom was having two other brothers that kept her busy. I felt that she was mine all mine. and this was the way she was for years. When she was six years old and ready to go to school the Lord told me to give her back to her mother. Well you know I thought I was hearing things, but most of all I didn't want to believe what I was hearing from the Lord. Oh what a struggle I went through with my self Lord she is nine to love, mine to help, mine to keep, she is mine Lord. You gave this baby to me. Over and over I would say, Lord don't you remember when I went out to her mother's house and parked the car and saw she had crawled out onto a iron porch two stories high she could fall through the open holes in the porch she was so small, it scared me to death. I ran up the stairs, no one was at home I grabbed her and ran out of the apartment building and sat in the car for along time shaking as I am

This Little Light Of Mine

right now recalling that instance as it was happening, this day and time. This was before she could walk. She crawled out onto that porch. Now I realize the Lord had her in the palm of his hand.(His Angel)

To obey the Lord I took her back to her mother's This was the hardest thing I have ever had to do in my life, but I obeyed the Lord. I took my her home to her mother but went to see her often I continued to do for and meet her needs as I did the same for her brothers.

My son had children by another girl in Summerville, New Jersey. They had two boys and two girls. I would drive from Queens, N.Y. over the Varazana Bridge to Goathals Bridge to Summerville, N.J. on Saturday every two weeks to see them, give them a trunk full of food 100 lb. bag of potatoes, fruit, spend the day with them take them to buy shoes and clothes and drive back to Jamaica, N.Y. alone.

Both set of children continue to grow up this little girl grow but at a slow pace, but she continued to be different. She was like the others. They had smart mouths and would be involved with books, school, games, and Television. They loved grandma too each one did and grandma loved them, but this little one was closer to grandma. This little one was so different she never asked you for anything, I saw that she had everything. She did not care too much for dolls, she was always afraid of balloons. I took her to Bear Mountain on a picnic I bought her a balloon I paid a large amount for the balloon the price was too much, but I wanted her to have it. I said this is a pretty balloon grandma wants you to play with it while we are here, after hugging her I handed it to her instead of tying it to her wrist she took it, and let it go, it went straight to heaven.

She never got angry about anything, unto this day she does no displ/y anger. She never got into a fight. Her brothers would take things from her and tease her but she never got angry. To this day I have never seen her angry or talk about anyone, nor curse, ok I hear you say she must not be human. Let me assure you she is alive a miracle from the Lord. A beautiful young woman God's Blessing to me. May I continue? She attended special schools and graduated High School. I was so proud of her and grateful to God for bringing her thus far.

I previously described her work Resume. During this time she continues to grow we celebrated her birthdays as a festival I loaded her with wrapped gifts mostly clothes. My Mom and Dad were getting older and required assistance so I wanted to move home to take care of them. I left my dear heart, home, church, friends, and went home to take care of my parents. My father lived to be ninety-four, My mother lived to be ninety-seven. After many, many, years the Lord blessed me with a second husband. A Godly man. I could not waite for my husband to meet my beautiful granddaughter, so we went to New York. We also attended the funeral of my dearest friend Oweda Harrison. She loved my Angel and my Angel loved her. My children called her Aunt Oweda. It was a lovely trip I spent time with my Angel. We returned home and had a wonderful marriage. My husband was sent from God. He was out of the ordinary. He loved me dearly and told me he loved me every day. We traveled, and he saw places he had never seen. He was assigned to guard Tokyo Rose in the Pacific World War 11. Traveled out of the States but did little in the States. In my first book I described in great detail our meeting, our marriage, and in Chapter 8 the death of my husband.

When my husband died I was totally devastated, I fell from a beloved Queen into another world of grief, and a broken heart. If there was a time I ever felt the presence of the Lord Jesus Christ I would have to say it was then. I am going to tell you the truth you might not believe me but the Lord came down here to me and was with me. He was giving me strength to wake up, I did that only with his help, after the funeral he came to comfort me, he was at my side, I wept and wept he was right there. He was there when people stop coming, and I was alone. I was alone even when people were around. I talked and moved out of habit for a long time. My doctor told me I had too much grief. I lost my brother that I loved dearly, my children's father, a dear friend who was like a sister to me, my daughter to lupus, my mother at ninety seven, and dad ninety four, my husband, and my son. I always believed your children are suppose to bury you, not you bury them.

I am glad God made time for it takes time to heal a broken heart, and to heal or take care of any thing you go through. God knew that and he gives us time to heal. Time to change our ways, time to turn our lives and come to him. He knows we need time. His time is not our time, He's always right on time, In His due time. After time passed I was still devastated that I had lost my husband and one day I had a phone call and it was my angel calling to tell me she was coming to live with me. I was so happy and full of joy, most of all I was thankful to know Jesus sent one of his angels to live with me.

I would like to tell you the angel the Lord sent to live with me has been with me many years. She is so precious to me, I love her so much, and I

This Little Light Of Mine

can't describe her in any other way then she was sent to me from heaven. A companion, a close friend, a granddaughter that I would call an angel sent from heaven. She is full of love, lovely to look at and sweet as sugar. She shows love to everyone, she is never mean, or angry with anyone. She always has a lovely smile on her face, she loves her grandmother, and her grandmother loves her dearly. She is a joy to me; she is a blessing to me. She and I go just about every place together wherever I go she goes. I love her to be with me and she loves to be with me.

What do you call that? I call it a blessing from heaven.

The tiny baby was sent to us to let us know Jesus came to earth human to feel pain, the sorrow, the trials we go through. He knows what to do for us to help us through our trials. For the Father knoweth what we have need of. The Love that was poured out and showed upon the baby was given back to me as an angel of a granddaughter.

We are free of arguments, anger, discord, situations arise we talk it out and come to a solution agreeable to both of us. We pray together, include the Lord in our decisions. We both ask the question would Jesus be please that is very important to us. We attend church together, we are sold out to Jesus, we get along very well, the Lord is pleased. In our house we serve the Lord and we are privilege to have the presence of the Lord here at all times. Our Bishop call's us cup cake and Twinkie.

My granddaughter will never have to worry about being without a home she loves this house and it will be hers when I go home to be with the Lord. At this time she has been on the same job for nine years, she loves her job. She will learn to drive soon. Thank you Lord for my Angel.

Isaiah 59: 21 As for me, this is my covenant with them, saith the Lord; My Spirit that is upon thee, and my words which I have put in thy mouth, shall not depart out of thy mouth, nor out of the mouth of thy seed, nor out of the mouth of thy seed's seed, saith the Lord, from henceforth and for ever.

Chapter 22

BLESSED ASSURANCE

In this day and time we live in it seems as if our survival is the most important thought we seem to concentrate upon. Our dying is not thought of. We have the idea since our mother and father lived to be in the late nineties, we take this as a sign that we will have that same privilege like a heritage from our family. Unfortunate this is not true, and it is a definite fact that in these times we are not guaranteed to live to see the evening sunset. Never has it been heard of mothers killing their infant babies, or their children ages three and up it seems we can not count on mothers love anymore. Young people are dying in rapid numbers laying on their own beds in their own home, killed by gun fired into the house. If they make it to school, they are being killed on the corner waiting for the bus, in the school, or on the way home. Our world is a time bomb ready to explode taking out anybody in the population. Unlike our forefathers who were led by God and his word to establish this country with equality for all people in mind. Our present leaders are controlled by satanic forces his seed is in their hearts. their actions are motivated by greed. The desire for power, hate, personal gratification, and vindication of old anguish, that has been laying dormant; and festering like a nasty cancer sore; the action of total destruction can accrue at any time, at any cost, meaning the destruction of the world and innocent people. Your objectivity and plans that you have made your life's goal can be terminated at any time in a second. Satan is out to kill us by any means; his job is to kill and destroy God's promises we have hide in our hearts. Satan tries to hinder us from our concentration on the word of God, by what the world does and

This Little Light Of Mine

desires. Our Lord tells us in his word; ***Fear him, which after he hath killed hath power to cast into hell, I say unto you, fear him. Luke 12: 5.***

I have come by here today to tell you that the Lord has not made provision for us who are in this world and not of it. As an answer to all our monumental what ifs and when. In his word He tells us, ***but seek ye first the kingdom of God and his righteousness, and all these things shall be added unto you. Matthew 6: 33-34.*** This is the first step if you want to receive this Blessed Assurance, and you should want it. To be forewarned is to be fore armed.

He in you the hope of glory is most valuable in your life, in this life and in the life to come. Colossians 1:27.
I must tell you, you must be born again. This means you will have to make a change in your heart, and mind, to believe in the Lord Jesus Christ. I would like to share this with you. I was giving a word of comfort to the Aunt of the young man that worked as a Security Guard in a nightclub that was shot last month it was all over the local news paper. The news paper stated the owner of the club gave a gun to the other security guard to shoot the Security guard that was killed. In talking to the aunt she told me the young security guard that was killed had given his heart to the Lord a month ago, and told her he was going to quit that job, he didn't want to work in a sinful place as that. She told me his last day to work was the Monday after he was killed. She told me he was baptized the Sunday before this happened and he was so happy he had excepted Christ as his personal Saviour, and was glad he was baptized. He told her he made up his mind to serve and live for the Lord.

For God so loved the world that he gave his only begotten Son that whosoever believeth on him should not perish, but have everlasting life. John 3:16. When you plant this seed into your heart and it falls on good ground it will produce good fruit to your soul. This is what the young man found out before it was too late. God is good and read that young man's heart, that he was sincere about serving the Lord and he is happy with his Lord and Saviour. After you have excepted the Lord as your Saviour you have the desire to learn the word. The word of God is a road map to lead us into righteousness. Whosoever keepeth the word in him verily is the love of God perfected: herby known we that we are in him.

Now that you have read this and realize what is more important to die in Christ with the hope of Eternal Life it is up to you to decide what it shall be. I have pored my heart out to you to remember it is not how you die, but if your name is written down in the Lambs book of life. That means you have excepted Jesus, repented of your sins, been baptized in water, turned from your sinful life, filled with the Holy Ghost, and is a follower of Jesus and his word.

The word of God tells us; ***But now being free from sin, and become servants to God ye have your fruit unto holiness, and the end everlasting life. For the wages of sin is death; and the gift of God is eternal life through Jesus Christ. Romans 6:22-23.***

Thank You Lord for this Blessed Assurance.

1 Samuel 15: 22 And Samuel said, Hath the Lord as great delight in burnt offerings and great delight in burnt sacrifice, as in obeying the voice of the Lord Behold, to obey is better than sacrifice, and to hearken than the fat of rams.

Chapter 23

To Obey Is To Win

This following is very personal to me I learned early in my life I was disobedient to my parents that cause my life to take a turn for the worst. I hope in your young life your parents always told you "you must obey your mother and father". I wonder if the advise is given to children of this day and age to obey their parents. I have some doubt because the parents are nothing but children themselves. I do feel sorry for the children and parents that have not received the teaching that they should have when they were growing up therefore they do not know what to teach their children. I can not say I didn't get the teaching for I did, but I was too young to realize there is a devil that seeks to kill and destroy you any way he can. Now you say you don't believe there is a devil that can destroy you in any way he can. I was raised up in church and loved God and was obedient to my parents and did the things that were pleasing to the Lord and the devil knew this, so he said I will put an end to this. He entered a man into my young life as a teenager, that was his follower and would do what he told him to do with me. This man I met at high school on the bus stop. He was skilled in talking to young girls that never went on a date before and was so dumb, a know nothing, who never been out of the house before (an old saying). All I knew was my family, going to school and church., this was my life. He was 11 years older then I was, had served in 2nd World War for four years, been all over the world, met many women, and was a matured man and a seasoned alcoholic.

Now I don't want you to think I wish to put all the blame on him, for I must tell you I was overwhelmed by his conversation, and (ate it up). My mom and dad told me he is too old for you, he is an alcoholic he does not mean you any good. I could continue with what they told me which they were absolutely right on target, but I was blinded and it seemed all the good raising I had went out the window. This could happen to your daughter or son as it happened to me with all the God I had in me. This was the target the devil aimed at (the God in me) this is his job to draw you away from God to him. Deception is one of his methods of gaining your attention to him. To break that bound of obedience to God and his word. I did not know what I was doing for I was truly innocent to the world of man, but guilty as I could be to the word of God. At the age I was I was weak to my flesh.

Ephesians 6: 1-3 Children, obey your parents in the Lord: for this is right. Honor thy father and mother: which is the first commandment with promise; That it may be well with thee, and thou mayest live long on the earth.

I married against my mother and fathers will and have paid for my disobedience all my life. Yes I have asked for forgiveness for my disobedience many times year after year, and believe the Lord has forgiven me, nevertheless God's word is the same forever and his word stands. The after effect of not obeying is destructive to your life, as it was to mine. I missed the opportunity to attend Howard University to continue my Music career, I played Concert Violin, I had three children after four years of marriage, I was a battered wife for nine years. When I could no longer tolerate being battered and mistreated I figured I put myself in this position and it was up to me to get myself out. I decided to get out of this situation by leaving the state. I had left him before, several times, but he always found us and forced me back home. I paid two lawyers for my divorce, but he convinced them I did not want to divorce him. Love had turned to hate and I began to fight back, this was to no avail. I just had to keep fighting him and he kept fighting me. I know this would have to stop, I thought he would eventually kill me getting away was my main goal. I bought a car and paid cash for it, and planed to leave town with my children. The day finally arrived when we leave for good. I put everything in the car and went back in the house to get my babies formula out of the refrigerator what happened then was not nice. The entire details are in my first book Chapter 1. As results I raised my three children alone with out a man. I worked and was the only support of my three children with the help of the Lord. I felt I had learned a great lesson and did everything I could to see that no man would get to me again to deceive me or my children, so I choose to live along, my children and I. I was determine not to disobey God's word again, once was enough.

Once your eyes are opened to light you can no longer be in darkness. I can not make the accusation of being perfect for that is far from being true for he alone is perfect, but I was very careful and mindful of Satan's attempt to over throw me in any way he could. I was aware of his tricks and games and stayed clear of them to avoid being trapped again. I want you to know no matter how well you try to live a sinless life Satan will be after you, but you have the Lord in you he will fight your battle. He tells us to put on the breastplate of righteousness, you are in Satan's territory and subject to failure, it is only in Christ are you saved and the winner. This is why in my house we will serve the Lord. If you have the determination to live and obey the Lord you will obey his word and base your life on living his word. It should matter to you what the word of God says and what the Lord say's to you this you must obey if you do you have a promise that goes along with it that is everlasting life with him.

In your life you might want to when in prayer to the Lord ask the Lord if you have committed any sin against him or his word to forgive you and mean it from your heart. I make it my business not to sin against the Lord but since the Lord reclaimed me and forgave me of my sins I ask for forgiveness from sin in my thoughts or deeds. It is my desire to see Jesus in peace and to see God with a pure heart. Love is the key and Obedience is the way.

About the Author:

This book is written by a Christian woman who loves the Lord and lives for the Lord. She was born to loving, God fearing parents who's father lived to be ninety four years of age. Her mother lived to be ninety seven years. Her mother and father were married seventy years. She was the oldest living of five brothers and one sister that died as a infant. She was raised humbly in a four room home with a out door toilet. She was a loving young girl who loved her mother, father and brothers. She was always ready to help older people as well as others who could not help themselves. As a young girl she fought her way to the public library though told she could not go. She engaged with children who would not let her go pass them. Her persistence allowed other children to go to that library and other places in the surrounding areas. This was the Brightwood area on the East side of Indianapolis, Indiana where she was raised.

It is good to be able to say you are a child of God. She was saved at the early age and played the piano for the young peoples' church activities. She held second chair in her High School orchestra in Crispus Attucks High School where she played the violin. She applied to Howard University and was excepted as a music major. She graduated from Indianapolis School for Practical Nursing. She took Indiana State Boards and passed to enter into her career of nursing. She holds Indiana, Ohio, and New York, Nurses License. She worked private duty in major hospitals in each State. She married and was the mother of two boys and one daughter. She raised her children without a father in the home, and without any financial support from anywhere. She moved to Jamaica, New York where she lived for thirty years. She worked for the New York City Department of Health. She was sent to various clinics in each area of the city. She attended Bethel Gospel Tabernacle under Sr. Pastor and Bishop Roderick R. Caesar located in Jamaica, N.Y. 110- 25 Guy R. Brewer Blvd. She went to the Bethel Bible Institute and Moody Accredited School of Theology for twelve years. Graduated with diploma's, degrees, and a teachers License. She taught Genesis in the institute. She has received Minister, Evangelist, and a Missionary License. She enrolled in Queensbourgh Community College in Bayside, New York and completed her nursing profession. She also attended New York University and graduated as a Audio Technician.

The Lord has anointed her to minister, teach, win souls, help others, and gave her a healing ministry to be an Evangelist. She is an anointed person that lives to spread the word. She willingly gives her testimony of what the Lord has done for her. Her testimony is to strengthen, encourage, and build faith in God by reaching souls for the Kingdom.

Due to her parents health issues and old age, she moved back to her hometown to care for them. The Lord gave her a husband and after six years of marriage, he died from a sudden heart attack. She remains a widow and continue to serve the Lord. The Lord anointed her to write her first book "A Miracle, Your Obedience My Testimony." and her second book, entitled, "This Little Light Of Mine." was written to reach souls for Christ. In this day and time, when people no longer want to hear the word of God, but want to do their own thing far from the word of God. This book is to be a light in darkness to show the way to receive salvation, a light to draw you close to the voice of Jesus, and a light to see the pathway that will lead you to your eternal home this should be your alternate goal.

Manufactured By: RR Donnelley
                     Momence, IL USA
                     November, 2010